The Family Game

A Situational Approach to Effective Parenting

The Family Game

A Situational Approach to Effective Parenting

Paul Hersey / Kenneth H. Blanchard

ADDISON-WESLEY PUBLISHING COMPANY
Reading, Massachusetts Menlo Park, California
London Amsterdam Don Mills, Ontario Sydney

Library of Congress Cataloging in Publication Data
Hersey, Paul.
  The family game.

    Includes bibliographical references and index.
    1. Parent and child. 2. Children--
  Management. 3. Family. I. Blanchard, Kenneth H.,
  joint author. II. Title.
  HQ772.H45   649'.1   77-92163
  ISBN 0-201-03068-3
  ISBN 0-201-03069-1 pbk.

Copyright (©) 1978 by Addison-Wesley Publishing Company, Inc.
Philippines copyright 1978 by Addison-Wesley Publishing Company, Inc.

All rights reserved. No part of this publication may be reproduced, stored in a retrieval system, or transmitted, in any form or by any means, electronic, mechanical, photocopying, recording, or otherwise, without the prior written permission of the publisher. Printed in the United States of America. Published simultaneously in Canada.

ISBN 0-201-03068-3-H
ISBN 0-201-03069-1-P
ABCDEFGHIJK-AL-798

To our children...

Glenna   *Scott*
Deborah   *Debbie*
David
Maureen
Michael
Garth

and to yours . . . there's room to write their names below. . .

PHOTO CREDITS

Cover photo and page 200, Diedra Delano Stead. Pages 2 and 146, Bruce Anderson. Pages 20, 46, Hank Harris. Page 74, Marshall Henrichs. Page 100, Marie Geggis. Page 116, Editeur officiel du Quebec. Page 166, Margie Blanchard. Page 186, Rafael Millán.

Contents

Why? 1

Chapter 1 *Parents in Blunderland* 3

What Is Leadership? 4 Successful versus Effective Parenting 5 Restrictive versus Permissive Child Rearing 7 The Approach Should Vary with the Situation 9 How This Book Can Help You as a Parent 11 Learning to Apply Theory 13 A Look at Your Present Leadership Style as a Parent 14

Chapter 2 *Different Strokes for Different Folks* 21

Directive Behavior and Supportive Behavior 21 Situational Leadership/Hersey and Blanchard 24 How Situational Leadership Works 29 Ineffective Parenting Styles 34 Willingness versus "Won'tness" 37 Supervising What Children Learn Outside the Home 40 Changing Leadership Style Appropriately 43

vii

Chapter 3 *Growing Winners* 47

    The Developmental Cycle 48 Positive Reinforcement: The Key to Growing Winners 66

Chapter 4 *What's Good for the Goose May Not be Good for the Gander* 75

    The Needs of Children 77 Goals or Reinforcers for Children 81 Needs/Goals and Parent Leadership Style 88 Need Levels and Goals Can Change 91 The Effect of Changing Needs on Leadership Style 95

Chapter 5 *Stopping Slippage* 101

    The Regressive Cycle 101 Some Things to Remember When Disciplining a Child 110

Chapter 6 *Monkey Business* 117

    Problem Ownership — Who's Got the Monkey? 117 Transactional Analysis 122 Transactional Analysis and Situational Leadership 134 The Problem-Solving Games Parents and Children Play 138

Chapter 7 *Parents Through the Looking Glass* 147

    The PARENT-Self 147 Determining Parent Style and Style Flexibility 149 Determining Style Adaptability 152 PARENT Profiles 156

Chapter 8   *Making It Work*   167

    What Does Our Self-Perception Mean?   167   Is It Too Late?   178   Team Building in the Family   181   Concluding Remarks   184

Bits and Pieces A   *PARENT-Other: Perception by Others (Parent Leadership Style)*   189

Bits and Pieces B   *Analysis and Rationale for the Twelve Situations from the PARENT-Self*   203

    References   221

    Index   227

Why?

For years we have been teaching in colleges and universities. At the same time we have been involved in countries throughout the world in training managers in a variety of organizations.

After conducting training in the behavioral sciences, we have gotten many letters from managers saying not only that what we taught was helpful to them on the job but that they found it meaningful in their parent-child relationships.

With that kind of reaction from people, it was felt that by writing this book specifically for the family, maybe we could help others be more effective in the important job of parenting. In fact, we have found this approach helpful in our own role as parents. We say "us" or "we" rather frequently throughout the book because, as the dedication indicates, we have eight children — and have the same desires you do to interact more effectively with them.

Our attempt is not to counsel or give answers to specific problems. It is to provide a framework that may help parents understand and work out solutions to the myriad of problems that face us all as parents today in a world of change. Our approach is summed up in the old saying:

Give a person a fish and he can eat for a day.
Teach a person *how* to fish and he will eat for a lifetime.

We can look at parenting as a constant problem or an ongoing challenge, as a win-lose competition or as a game we can all win — The Family Game.

Paul Hersey   *Ken Blanchard*

1 • Parents in Blunderland

The other day, while out for a walk, we spotted our ten-year-old neighbor A. J. sitting glumly on his front steps, chin in hands. He looked very bored. "What's the matter, A. J.?" we called over.

"There's nothing to do," A. J. replied. "There's no Little League practice today and the playground is closed. I don't know what to do."

A. J.'s dilemma started us thinking. Were we ever bored as kids? We couldn't remember many times — we always seemed to have something to do.

Why the difference? Why do today's young people seem so apathetic at school as well as at play? Why the increasing number of attempted and successful suicides at early ages?

In trying to pinpoint the difference, we realized that as kids we had no one to blame for boredom but ourselves. We had no Little League, no recreation directors. The responsibility for entertaining ourselves was ours alone. If, for example, we wanted to play baseball, we first had to find a place to play. This generally meant getting together a group of neighborhood kids to scout out a vacant lot, get permission from the owner to use it, and then begin the job of clearing off rocks and raking the field. We had no coaches, no uniforms, no fancy equipment. (In fact, for years we thought a baseball was black rather than white — we'd never seen one that wasn't held together by tape. And one thing that guaranteed a spot on the team was owning a bat — they were really scarce. If one broke, nails were hammered into it for support.)

When it came to learning the skills of the game, we were pretty much on our own. We taught one another what we picked up from the "big kids," and when we began to feel like "hot stuff," we challenged a group of kids a few blocks away. When we beat them, we would challenge another group a few more blocks away. Pretty soon we had a Little League of our own going.

But who did the planning? The organizing? The motivating? The kids, of course. Who does it today? The Little League director, the parent coaches — anyone but the kids. All they have to do is show up for the game. They have beautiful fields, uniforms, even refreshment stands. And undoubtedly they have better skills than earlier generations. But haven't they lost something as well? Have we adults taken away their opportunities for leadership, creativity, and responsibility? Have we deprived them of the chance to experience and deal with anxiety and frustration?

In this book we intend to focus on these and other questions and help you as parents, develop alternatives to your traditional jobs of planning, organizing, motivating, and controlling the lives of young people. Our goal is to help develop independent, self-motivated children who can take charge of their own lives. We believe it sometimes takes more love simply to stand back and let your kids "go it on their own" than to guide their every move. The frustrations and anxieties they encounter now will help them cope more effectively with problems later in life.

What Is Leadership?

Parenting is really a form of leadership.[1] Whenever someone tries to influence the behavior of another individual or group, whether in the home, neighborhood, school, or office, leadership is occurring. Thus, leadership is an influence process that everyone engages in at one time or another. Parents, for example, assume a leadership role when they try to have an impact on their children.

The emphasis in this book is on the parent/child relationship.

The concepts apply not only to a parent attempting to influence the behavior of a child, but also the reverse — a child attempting to influence the behavior of a parent. The individual making the attempt is always the *potential leader*, and the person he or she is trying to influence is the *potential follower*, no matter what their "real" relationship may be (e.g., boss/subordinate, child/parent, parent/child). That is what the Family Game is all about — influencing behavior.

Successful versus Effective Parenting

As parents, it's helpful to understand that *successful* parenting is not synonymous with *effective* parenting. Let's explore how they differ.

Any time a parent tries to have some effect on the behavior of a child, the parent is attempting leadership. The child's response to this attempted leadership can be successful or unsuccessful, depending on the extent to which the child does what the parent wants. It's by no means an either/or situation. The parent's success could range from very successful to very unsuccessful.

For example, suppose a mother wants to get her son, Johnny, to clean up his room. The mother's attempted leadership would be considered successful if Johnny cleans up his room. If, however, Johnny not only cleans up his room but also reorganizes his bureau drawers and his closet, his mother may consider herself more successful than she had anticipated. On the other hand, if Johnny chooses to throw a temper tantrum and mess up his room even further, his mother is less successful than expected.

Let's assume that the mother's leadership attempt is successful. In other words, Johnny responds by cleaning up his room. This behavior alone, however, does not tell us how *effective* her leadership attempt is. If Johnny is resentful and only cleans up his room because his mother can punish him if he doesn't, then she has been successful but not effective. Johnny has responded as his mother intended because she has control of rewards and punishment — not because he sees his own needs and desires being met by doing this task.

On the other hand, if Johnny cleans up his room because he wants to — it makes sense to him and he loves and respects his mother — then his mother has been effective as well as successful. Johnny is willing to cooperate because he feels his mother's request is reasonable and necessary.

Thus, success has to do with how a child behaves, while effectiveness involves not only behavior but attitudes and feelings as well. Effective leadership, like successful leadership, can range from very effective to ineffective. If parents are interested only in success, they tend to emphasize their power as parents and only care that their children do what they want them to do *now*. However, if parents are effective, they get the behavior they want and, in addition, generate feelings of respect and trust in their relationship with their children.

The difference between successful and effective often explains why children behave very differently when their parents aren't looking over their shoulders. For example, if the Youngs are both successful and effective with their teenage children, their children will accept family goals as their own. If Frank and Sally Young leave for the weekend, their children will behave no differently than if they were there. If, however, the Youngs continually emphasize getting the behavior they want without taking into consideration the feelings and opinions of their children, it is likely they maintain order only because of the rewards and punishments they control. Their return from a trip might very well be greeted by havoc, chaos, and evidence of wild parties.

Sometimes, of course, all that is important in parenting is successfully influencing our children's behavior *right now* — for example, if they are playing too close to a busy street. But if we are interested in a more lasting influence, it is important to concentrate on being both successful and effective. If this is done, we will have influence on our children even when we're not on the scene.

Take the situation of Dorothy and Ron Irwin. They were afraid their teenage daughter Roslyn was so crazy about her boyfriend that she would do something foolish, something contrary to their religious and moral beliefs. Motivated by these strong concerns, they picked her up after school every day, didn't permit her to go to any parties, and closely supervised her every move. As you might imagine, with that kind of supervision Roslyn kept out of trouble. But for how long did that "good behavior" last? As is not uncommon with children who have been overcontrolled, it lasted until Roslyn left home for college, where she engaged in all kinds of premarital sexual activity — almost as if to get even with her parents for their mistrust and restrictiveness. So, while Roslyn's parents were successful in the short run, they failed miserably in the long run. Away from their watchful eye, Roslyn went off the deep end.

If Roslyn's parents had sat down and talked with her in a rational, unemotional way when they first became concerned about her relationship with her boyfriend, they might have set the stage for a more lasting influence. Suppose, at that time, they had shared with Roslyn their concerns and explained why it was important to them for her not to engage in premarital sexual relations. Treating her as the adult she was soon to become, her parents might have tried to get her to begin to think about the future and what kind of person she wanted to become. They could have arranged discussions for her with their minister or a sex education counselor. Throughout this process, Roslyn could have been an active participant, sharing her feelings and thoughts with her parents. Eventually, even her boyfriend could have become involved in the discussions. Roslyn's parents, by listening and responding to their daughter's attitudes and feelings, could have been both successful and effective in the long run.

Restrictive versus Permissive Child Rearing

In describing the difference between successful and effective parenting, we implied that there are various styles (ways of influencing children) we can use in our child-rearing efforts. Over the years, parents and writers in the field of child rearing have been involved in a search for a "best" style, one that would work in most situations. Some parents have opted for restriction; others believe permissiveness is the only way to raise children. The result has been a polarization of approaches with the nod for the "best" approach swinging back and forth between the two extremes. This polarization has resulted in the belief that restrictive and permissive are either/or ways of raising children. While the initial swing from the restrictive to permissive philosophy seemed irrevocable, in recent years there has been a growing call for a return to a more restrictive child-rearing philosophy.

The restrictive approach is the traditional, authoritarian style of child rearing. It emphasizes parental direction, the development of discipline, respect for authority, and awareness of the rights of others. The permissive approach is the more nondirective, supportive style of child rearing. It stresses love, affection, understanding, and the satisfaction of the child's needs.

The differences in the two approaches may be traced to assumptions parents make about where their power comes from and what kids are like.[2] The restrictive child-rearing philosophy is often based on the assumption that parents can make their kids do things simply because they are their parents. This is called "position power," the extent to which parents perceive that they have rewards, punishments, or sanctions that can be brought to bear on their children. If their child asks, "Why do I have to do that?" the answer is almost automatic: "Because we said so!"

Parents who emphasize their position power often are interested in being successful only in the present; they care how their children behave, not how they feel. The philosophy also reflects certain assumptions about what kids are like. Restrictive parents often feel that kids are basically lazy and irresponsible; they will be responsible, disciplined, and show respect for others only if motivated by the "stick of fear" or the "carrot of goodies." For example, "If you're bad at Aunt Martha's, you're going to get the spanking of your life!" or, "If you're good today, I'll take you to the movies tomorrow." These parents assume that, unless closely supervised, their kids will get into trouble. Such parents treat their children as if they were unwilling and unable to discipline themselves or run their own lives.

The permissive child-rearing philosophy assumes that the power parents have is earned from their children. Their kids' willingness to cooperate gives parents their power. This is called "personal power," the extent to which children feel good about and respect their parents and accept their parents' goals as their own. As A. S. Neill argues in *Summerhill*, "to impose anything by authority is wrong. The child should not do anything until he comes to the opinion — his own opinion — that it should be done."[3]

Parents who emphasize their personal power rather than position power often seem to be interested only in being effective in the present; they care how their children feel, not how they behave. Parents using this approach base their actions on a different set of assumptions about kids. They feel that children are better off if they regulate their own activities as much as possible; if given the opportunity, children will be responsible, self-disciplined, and respectful of others. They believe their children can be trusted to make decisions for themselves and run their own lives.

Once the restrictive and permissive approaches to child rearing were clearly identified, the debate began over which was the better way to raise children. This discussion has now become unproductive. The advocates of each approach can produce shining examples of their successes as well as glaring examples of their opponents' failures. Thus, the debate has only intensified the conflict about what is "right" and "wrong" in child-rearing approaches. As a result, we have swung wildly from one extreme to another for decades, leaving parent and expert alike confused and discouraged. The question now to be answered is: Is there really one "best" approach to child rearing?

The Approach Should Vary with the Situation

Implied support for the idea that there is no one best approach to child rearing has begun to appear in books and articles on the subject. "Informed permissive" is the label given to one approach that departs from the either/or philosophies. As Francis L. Ilg and Louis Bates Ames explain:

The restrictive parent tends to say no to almost everything; the permissive parent tends to say yes to almost anything; and the informed permissive parent tends to say yes and no, depending on the child's stage of development and what can be reasonably expected and not expected of him.[4]

Even Benjamin Spock, who received much of the credit as well as the blame for suggesting a more permissive approach to child rearing as far back as the middle 1940s, is now saying in his recently revised version of *Baby and Child Care* that different situations call for different responses:

Moderate strictness — in the sense of requiring good manners, prompt obedience, orderliness — is not harmful to children so long as the parents are basically kind and so long as the children are growing up happy and friendly . . . parents who incline to an easygoing kind of management, who are satisfied with casual manners as long as the child's attitude is friendly, or who happen not to be particularly strict — for instance, about promptness or neatness — can also raise children who are considerate and cooperative, as long as the parents are not afraid to be firm about those matters that do seem important to them.[5]

Even people who recognize that restrictive and permissive child-rearing practices are not either/or approaches are often still uncomfortable without some guidance; they want to be told how to act. And yet it has become clear that while a certain prescribed child-rearing approach might work in some families with some children, it may completely fail in others. This is true because children vary significantly, even within the same age group, according to personality, their reaction to the home situation, and the like.

The concept of a *situational approach to child rearing* might be stated as follows: *Effective parents are those who can adapt their approach to child rearing to meet the unique needs of each* of their children and the particular situation or environment in which their family exists. If their children are different, they must be treated differently.

This certainly sounds reasonable, but where does a parent go from here? How do you determine the right strategy for a given situation? Even parents who realize that they must adapt their style to fit the needs of each child are frustrated by the conclusion that this child-rearing approach "depends on the situation." They need to first see *how* child-rearing methods depend on the situation before they can decide *what* approach tends to be effective *when*.

How This Book Can Help You as a Parent

Recognizing this dilemma, we have been working for the last decade to develop a practical, easy-to-understand theory that makes sense and can help us as parents answer the how, what, and when questions about child rearing. Our objective was to come up with a theory that would help parents make effective day-to-day decisions on how to handle various situations involving children. The results of our efforts, Situational Leadership, provide a framework for discussing the complex business of raising kids. The theory will be presented more completely in the chapters that follow.

Situational Leadership can help us develop knowledge and skills in three areas: understanding past behavior; predicting future behavior; and directing, changing, and controlling behavior. If we become comfortable with these skills, we feel we will become more effective in positively influencing the behavior of our children.

Understanding Past Behavior

Why do children behave as they do? To be able to influence our kids, we must first know why they act in certain ways. Understanding past behavior is the initial step in this direction.

What motivates children? What produces their characteristic behaviors? Much of what has been written in the child-rearing field focuses on these questions. Literally hundreds of different classifications have been used to describe how kids interact with other people. We can say a child is hyperactive or shy or aggressive or cooperative. All of these are useful classifications for communicating to others the way in which a child or group of children behaves.

Predicting Future Behavior

Although understanding past behavior is important for effective parent skills, it is not enough by itself. If we are raising children, it is also essential to be able to predict how they are going to behave today, tomorrow, next week, and next month under similar as well as changing circumstances. Therefore, the second level of knowledge and skill that parents need is predicting future behavior.

Directing, Changing, and Controlling Behavior

Finally, we need to develop skills in directing, changing, and controlling behavior. When we talk about "controlling" behavior, many parents express some alarm. "Do you mean we're supposed to manipulate behavior?" they ask. Control and manipulation have certain negative connotations today, particularly in the minds of young people. Our response is that if we are concerned about the behavior of our children and the kinds of values they develop, we are concerned about controlling behavior. If we are concerned about our children — their cohesiveness, their commitment to one another, their relationship with us — then we are concerned about controlling behavior. If we are concerned about their participating or not participating in certain activities, then we are concerned about controlling behavior. The label isn't important. Call it anything! Perhaps you can think of a better word — facilitating, training, having an impact, whatever. But remember, if we accept the leadership role of a parent, we accept with it the responsibility for having an impact on the behavior of our children. And to be effective in carrying out that role, we need to develop the knowledge and skills we've just outlined. The goal of this book is to help us do just that.

Learning to Apply Theory

Our objective in these discussions is to share with you information and concepts from the behavioral sciences that can help us interact more effectively with our children; therefore, your job and our job is to learn to apply these concepts in our childrearing efforts. A few cautions, however, are worth mentioning before we move ahead.

Learning to apply the behavioral sciences is much like learning anything; for example, how do we learn to hit a baseball or make a perfect soufflé? We learn by practice, by actually doing what we are attempting to learn. We'll never learn to hit a baseball or make a soufflé merely by reading books, or even by watching the experts in action. All that will do is give us more conceptual knowledge. Psychologists define learning as a change in behavior — being able to do something differently than we were able to do it before. So, in reading and watching others, all we accomplish is perhaps a change in our knowledge or attitudes. If we want to make something a real learning situation, we have to "try on" the new skill.

Another thing to keep in mind as you move ahead in this book: How do you feel the first time you attempt something new, something significantly different? If you're like most, you feel anxious, nervous, and uncomfortable. This is to be expected. Don't let it deter you.

Learning to use behavioral science concepts is the same thing as learning any other new skill. Much of what you read in this book may have an impact on your knowledge and attitudes, but it only becomes relevant if you are willing to try out the new behaviors. If you are, you should recognize that the first time you try a new pattern of behavior, you're going to feel ill at ease and uncomfortable. We have to go through this "unfreezing" if we want to learn.

Further, it's important to remember that the probability of getting a solid hit the "first time at bat" is low. The first time you attempt to behave differently because of a new theory, you will probably be more effective using your old style of behavior than the new one (although, in the long run, the new style may have a higher probability of success). This is why parents so often become discouraged when they first try to put into practice some new child-rearing technique they have read. As a result of their initial failure, they begin to respond negatively to everything they read. "How can we accept these theories?" they ask. "These ideas don't work in the real world." All of us have to recognize that, just like hitting a baseball, behavioral science theory takes practice. The first few times up, the probability of success is quite low. But the more we practice, the more we attempt to find out how well we are doing, the more successful we will be.

A Look at Your Present Leadership Style as a Parent

Since parents don't all try to influence their children in the same way, we think it's important to gather some information about how you think you behave *now* in various child-rearing situations. To find out more about your own leadership style as a parent, we suggest that you read the directions below and respond to the twelve items that follow. These items comprise the PARENT-Self Perception Questionnaire.[6]

PARENT-Self

Assume you are involved in each of the following twelve child-rearing situations. Read each item carefully. Think about what you as a parent have done in each circumstance. Then circle the letter of the alternative action choice which you think most closely describes your parent behavior in the situation presented. Circle only one choice.

This is not a test or quiz. Respond to the items according to how *you have behaved* in the past when faced with situations similar to those described, or according to the way you think *you would behave*.

Respond to the items in order; that is, do item 1 before you do item 2, and so on. Do not spend too much time; respond to each question as if you were responding to a real-life situation. Don't go back over the questionnaire; go with your original responses.

PARENT-Self

Situation 1

Your children are not responding lately to the friendly ways you have been asking them to help around the house. Their chores are not getting done and their rooms are a mess.

Alternative Actions

A. Direct and closely supervise the completion of their chores.
B. In a pleasant and friendly manner continue to encourage their helping around the house.
C. Discuss the situation with your children and then make sure they complete their chores.
D. Don't do anything now; assume their behavior will improve.

Situation 2

Your children are getting better in doing their homework each evening. You have been strict in checking to see that all their assigned work has been done. Reports from school show improvement.

Alternative Actions

A. Share with them how pleased you are with the results, but continue to make sure the assignments are completed.
B. Since they have improved, let them do the work on their own now.
C. Express your approval and be available for help as needed.
D. Continue to direct and supervise their homework.

Situation 3

Your children are unable to resolve a conflict with some of their friends. You have normally not interfered in these situations. In the past they have seemed to take such conflicts in stride and have worked out the problems themselves. This time this approach is not working.

Alternative Actions

A. Discuss the problem with your children and direct their efforts at problem solving.
B. Let them work it out themselves as they have done in the past.
C. Tell your children how to solve the conflict and make sure they do it.
D. Encourage your children to resolve the conflict and be supportive of their efforts.

PARENT-Self (continued)

Situation 4

You are considering some rearranging in your son's room. Lately he has demonstrated responsibility around the house and he is presently taking good care of his room. Recently he talked with you about changing his room arrangement.

Alternative Actions

A. Participate with your son in deciding about the rearrangement and be supportive of his efforts.
B. Decide what rearranging has to be done and then direct the completion of those changes.
C. Allow your son to decide how he would like to alter his room. Let him do it on his own.
D. Discuss with your son your ideas for rearranging, but make the final decisions yourself.

Situation 5

The behavior of your daughter has been deteriorating during the last few months. She has been uncooperative and inconsiderate to family members. She has continually needed reminding to do her household chores on time. "Laying down the law" and making sure she is helpful and cooperative have helped in the past.

Alternative Actions

A. Consider this a stage she is going through and don't do anything now.
B. Listen to her and find out what she thinks about her behavior, but see that she gets her chores done and shows respect toward family members.
C. Act quickly and firmly to correct and redirect her behavior.
D. Sit down and discuss the situation with her and find out what she thinks ought to be done; take no direct steps.

Situation 6

You have just returned from the hospital where you have been recovering from an illness. During your absence the family situation has been running smoothly. Your spouse at home has been closely supervising the children. You want to maintain good behavior, but also want to get the children involved in family decision making.

PARENT-Self (continued)

Alternative Actions

A. Do what can be done to make your children feel important and involved.
B. Continue with close supervision and guidance.
C. Let the children direct their own behavior.
D. Begin to let the children have some role in family decision making, but be careful that decisions made are carried out.

Situation 7

Due to a new job, work around the house needs to be shared in a different way. Your children understand the problem and have made suggestions on how they could help. They have usually done their chores in the past.

Alternative Actions

A. Tell your children what their new jobs are and then closely supervise the completion of those jobs.
B. Participate with the family in deciding new ways to share the expanding responsibilities and support their cooperative efforts.
C. Be willing to make new work assignments as recommended by your children, but make sure that everyone is doing his or her share.
D. Just let the assuming of new responsibilities emerge; take no definite action.

Situation 8

Your children are behaving in responsible ways and get along well with each other and their parents. Yet you feel somewhat unsure about your lack of supervision of their activities.

Alternative Actions

A. Stop worrying about it and continue to leave them alone.
B. Decide what action to take and then discuss your decision with the children.
C. Take steps to direct and supervise their behavior.
D. Discuss the situation with your children and reach an agreement on action.

PARENT-Self (continued)

Situation 9

Your children are way behind in some fall clean-up that you asked them to do around the outside of the house. Often they don't show up when they are supposed to work. When they do appear, rather than working, they play and fool around.

Alternative Actions

A. Let the children continue to set their own work schedule. They know what has to be done and they'll eventually get around to it.
B. Ask the children why the job is not getting done and listen for any suggestions they may have, but supervise the completion of the job.
C. Direct and closely supervise the children until the job is done.
D. Discuss the situation with the children in a friendly manner.

Situation 10

Your son, usually able to take some responsibility for handling money, is not responding to a change in spending caused by the family's present financial situation.

Alternative Actions

A. Allow your son involvement in determining the necessary spending limits and be supportive of his suggestions.
B. Restate the new limitations to your son and then closely supervise his spending.
C. Avoid confrontation by not saying anything about his spending; leave the situation alone and assume it will all work out.
D. Discuss the problem with your son and answer questions about the family's money situation, but see that he follows the new plan.

Situation 11

Your teenage daughter has been conscientious about doing her homework and helping around the house without supervision. Now that she is beginning to date she seems to be on the phone much of the time and her schoolwork and chores are suffering.

PARENT-Self (continued)

Alternative Actions

A. Restrict her phone calls and supervise the completion of her homework and chores around the house.
B. Discuss the new development with your daughter and give her an opportunity to participate in the solving of the problem.
C. Discuss the situation with your daughter and get her suggestions; then you develop a plan that she will have to follow.
D. Don't intervene now; see if she realizes the problem and does something to correct it.

Situation 12

Recently, your children seem to be upset with each other. Over the last several years they have gotten along well together. During that period of time all the children have done extremely well in school and have taken responsibility for their chores around the house. They have worked in harmony together on family projects and have been able to settle any difficulties on their own.

Alternative Actions

A. Talk with your children about the situation and then decide yourself what needs to be done to remedy it.
B. Don't interfere; wait to see if the children work it out themselves.
C. Act quickly and firmly to correct and redirect.
D. Discuss the situation with your children and be supportive.

You have just completed the PARENT-Self Perception Questionnaire. We hope you have gained some insights that will be useful in analyzing your leader behavior as a parent. In Chapters 2 through 6, we introduce some theories and concepts that make it possible for you to understand and interpret your responses to the PARENT-Self. It's important to read those chapters before you score your PARENT-Self in Chapter 7. In that chapter, "Parents through the Looking Glass," you will have an opportunity to receive feedback on what your PARENT-Self scores mean and on what those scores suggest for your self-development.

2 • *Different Strokes for Different Folks*

"Different strokes for different folks" is a phrase that aptly describes effective parenting. Effective parents are those who can change their behavior depending on the situation and the child involved. If that is true, then what are the various parenting styles and how can parents determine when to use which style? That is what this chapter is all about.

Directive Behavior and Supportive Behavior

Most of the child-rearing activities of parents can be classified into two distinct behavioral categories: directive behavior and supportive behavior.[1]

Directive behavior involves one-way communication; the parent spells out the child's role and tells the child what to do, where to do it, when to do it, and how to do it. If there is more than one child, it may mean directing who's to do what, where, when, and how.

Supportive behavior involves two-way communication; the parent listens to the child, provides support, encouragement, positive "strokes," and helping behaviors for the child.

Parental leadership tends to vary considerably. Some parents mainly direct the activities of their children to get things done (as in the restrictive child-rearing approach), while other parents concentrate on providing support and encouragement, but little direction for their children (as in the permissive child-rearing approach). Still other parent behavior is characterized by

21

a combination of directive and supportive behavior or, alternatively, by little direction or support of any kind. These four basic parenting styles contain various amounts of both directive and supportive behavior. Any of the four basic styles shown in Figure 1 may be effective or ineffective depending on the situation.

As Figure 1 illustrates, a shorthand labeling of the four parent leadership styles clarifies what behaviors are associated with each style *when they are used appropriately.*

1. High directive and low supportive parent behavior will be referred to as "telling" (S1). This style is called "telling" because it is characterized by one-way communication in which the parent defines the roles of the children and tells them what, how, when, and where to do various tasks. *"Johnny, clean off the front walk and porch by 4:00 this afternoon. First, sweep them off, then put what you have collected in the garbage."*
2. High directive and high supportive parent behavior will be referred to as "selling" (S2). This style is called "selling" because most of the direction is still provided by the parent. Yet he or she also attempts, through two-way communication that permits the child to ask questions and provides support and encouragement, to get the child to psychologically buy into decisions that the parent feels have to be made. *"Johnny, we have company coming today at 4:00, and the front walk and porch are a mess. I want you to clean them off this afternoon — the house will look so much better. Do you have any questions on how to do that job?"*
3. High supportive and low directive parent behavior will be referred to as "participating" (S3). This style is called "participating" because the parent and child now share in decision making through two-way communication. The child has the ability and knowledge to share ideas about how the problem can be solved and agrees with his or her parent on what needs to be done.
"Johnny, we have company coming today at 4:00 and the front walk and porch are a real mess. It makes it look as if we don't care about our house. What do you think we can do about it? Do you have any suggestions?"

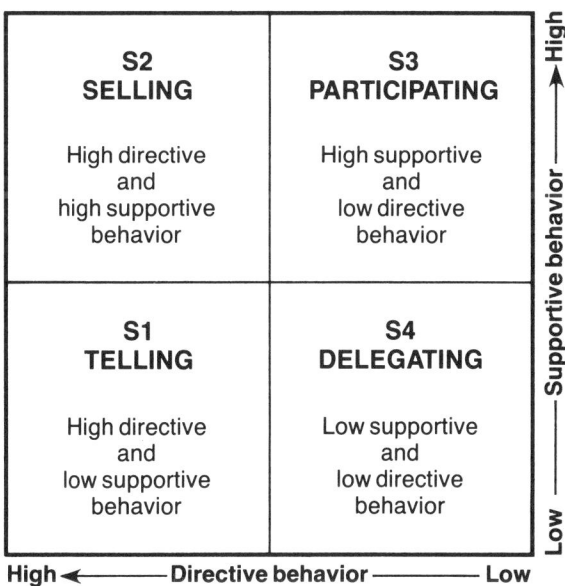

Figure 1. Basic parent styles.

4. Low supportive and low directive parent behavior will be referred to as "delegating" (S4). This style is called "delegating" because, even though the parent may still define the problem or what needs to be done, the child is now permitted to "run the show" and decide on the when, where, and how of doing the task. He or she now has both the ability and the motivation to work alone successfully. *"Johnny, we have company coming today at 4:00, and I know you recognize that the front walk and porch don't look right for company. Why don't you take care of that situation?"*

In all four cases the parent identifies the task to be done but varies the amount of direction and support given to the child. To determine the appropriate blend of these two behaviors and thus the appropriate parenting style, we need to look at the maturity of the child in a given situation. That's the key to effective leadership.

Situational Leadership/Hersey and Blanchard

Situational Leadership[2] is based on an interplay among (1) the amount of direction and supervision (directive behavior) parents give, (2) the amount of support and encouragement (supportive behavior) parents provide, and (3) the "maturity" level their child or children exhibit in a certain aspect of their lives.

Thus, while a number of environmental factors can influence and determine the style a parent should use in a particular situation, the emphasis in Situational Leadership is on the behavior of parents and their children. It is generally agreed that the relationship between a parent(s) and a child(ren) is the most crucial factor in any family environment. Children are vital, not only because individually or as a group they accept or reject their parents, but also because the relationship between parents and their children often determines the kind of relationship that develops between the parents as husband and wife.

Thus, we are not suggesting that influence is a one-way street, from parent to child. While our examples tend to emphasize the parent attempting to influence the child, the concepts presented in Situational Leadership apply to any influence situation, whether the person be your parent, spouse, child, or friend.

Level of Maturity

In applying Situational Leadership to child rearing, it is important to consider the child's level of maturity. Maturity is defined by the willingness and ability of children to take responsibility for directing their own behavior. *Level of maturity should be considered only in relation to a specific aspect of a child's life — a specific area in which his or her parent wants to have some influence.* In other words, a child is not mature or immature in any total sense. Children exhibit varying degrees of maturity in different aspects of their lives. Thus, Susie, a young baby, may be good at eating the food that her mom fixes her but very unpredictable about settling down for a nap in the afternoon. Pablo, a ten-year-old boy, may be very mature about helping his father around the house but very irresponsible when it comes to doing homework. Mary Eliza, a teenage girl, may be very responsible in caring for her clothes but very lax about getting home on time from dates. In addition to judging the level of maturity of each of the children within a family, a parent may have to judge the maturity of the children as a group, particularly when they are interacting or playing together. Thus, parents with more than one child may find they have to watch their children more closely and give them more direction when they are playing together rather than separately.

The Basic Concept of Situational Leadership

To determine what leadership style we should use with a child, we must do several things.

First, we need to decide what areas of our child's life we would like to influence. Those areas often vary according to the child's age. For example, if a child is a baby, parents usually are most interested in such areas as eating, sleeping, toilet training, and dressing. For the child seven to ten years of age, parents are likely to change their emphasis to cleaning one's room, doing chores, respect for adults, and interpersonal relations. With teenagers, parents might be most concerned about schoolwork, sex, drugs, and finances. Whatever the age, though, we must decide what aspects of our child's life we want to influence before we can begin to determine the appropriate leadership style to use.

Once this decision has been made, the next step is to determine the maturity level of the child in each of the selected areas. We need to ask ourselves questions about the child's ability or skill as well as willingness or motivation to direct his or her own behavior.

The final step is deciding which of the four leadership styles (see Figure 1) would be appropriate with our child in each of these areas.

Situational Leadership suggests that when working with a child who is low in maturity in a particular area, a directive style has the best chance of success. As the child's level of maturity increases, less direction is needed and the child can be given increased responsibility in certain areas. As he or she shows greater willingness and ability to take on responsibilities, our withdrawal of direction and control should be reinforced by an increase in supportive behavior. If a parent reduces directive behavior and increases supportive behavior too soon, however, the child may misinterpret this as permissiveness and thus feel free to act as he or she pleases. Eventually, as the child reaches a moderate to high level of maturity, less support from the parents is needed. The child begins to mature psychologically and is able to direct his or her own activities. Internal direction takes the place of external direction. By reducing close supervision and increasing delegation at this time, parents can demonstrate their trust and confidence in their children.

We will be discussing this whole developmental process in much more depth in the next chapter. At this point, though, we want to emphasize that Situational Leadership focuses on the appropriateness or effectiveness of parent styles at particular maturity levels. This relationship is illustrated by a bell-shaped curve placed over the four leadership quadrants, as shown in Figure 2.

Now, for those of you who find diagrams frightening, *relax* and give us a chance to explain what it all means.

Style of Parent versus Maturity of Child

Figure 2 shows the relationship between maturity and the parent styles to be used as a child moves from immaturity to maturity. Keep in mind that the figure represents two different concepts. The appropriate leadership style *(Style of Parent)* for given levels of child maturity is represented by the bell-shaped curve running through the four leadership quadrants — Telling (S1), Selling (S2), Participating (S3), and Delegating (S4). The maturity level of the child being influenced *(Maturity of Child)* is shown below the leadership model as a continuum ranging from immaturity to maturity. Maturity is a question of degree. Figure 2 establishes some benchmarks of maturity by dividing the maturity continuum into four areas, or levels: low maturity will be referred to as maturity level M1; low to

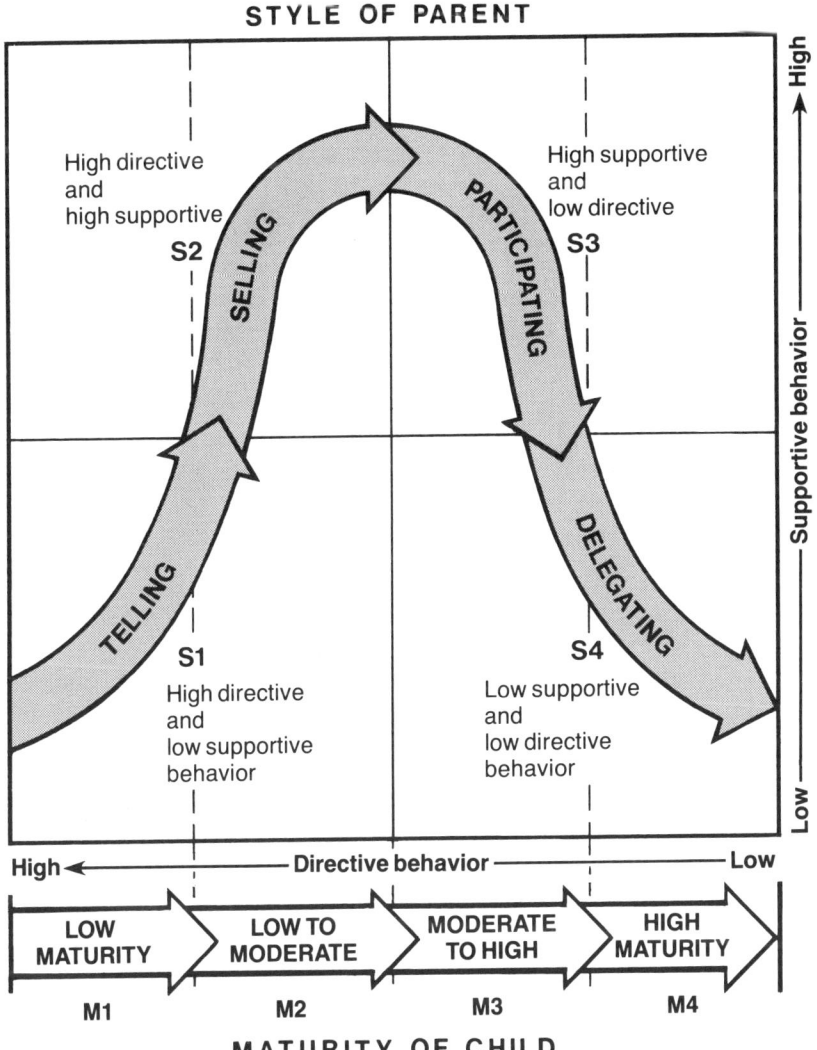

Figure 2. Situational Leadership.

moderate maturity will be called maturity level M2; moderate to high maturity will be called M3; and high maturity will be called M4.

Components of Maturity

The key to effective parenting is to identify the *maturity level* of our child and then bring to bear the appropriate leadership. If that is true, how can parents get a better handle on what maturity actually means in child rearing?

When we talk about the maturity of children, we need to consider two components: their ability or skill, and their willingness or motivation.

Ability is a child's skill in doing something. Children who have ability in a particular area have the skill, knowledge, and experience to do tasks in that area without direction from others.

"My best subject in school is math. I can work on my own in math without much help from the teacher or Mom and Dad."

Willingness is a child's motivation to do something. Children who are willing to do something in a particular area think that area is important (a "turn on") and display self-confidence and good feelings about themselves. They do not need extensive "patting on the back" or encouragement to get things done.

"I really enjoy working around the yard. It turns me on. Mom and Dad don't have to get after me to do that kind of thing."

There are, of course, four combinations of these factors:

1. Children who are *neither able nor willing* to take responsibility for their own behavior in a particular area. These children are considered to be low in maturity (M1).
   "I'm not interested in that, and besides no one ever really taught me how to do it right. I always seem to mess the job up."

2. Children who are *willing but not able* to take responsibility for their own behavior in a particular area. These children are considered to be low to moderate in maturity (M2). *"I would really like to start doing that, but I haven't learned how to yet."*
3. Children who are *able but not willing* to take responsibility for their own behavior in a particular area. These children are considered to be moderate to high in maturity (M3). *"Sure I know how to do that, but it's not something that interests me. I'd rather do other things."*
4. Children who are *both willing and able* to take responsibility for their own behavior in a particular area. These children are considered to be high in maturity (M4). *"That's something that really excites me. I feel confident and do it well. I don't need help from anyone."*

The highest level of maturity for a child (in our terms) is when that child is willing and able to do something (combination 4). The lowest level maturity is when a child is unwilling and unable to do something (combination 1).

How Situational Leadership Works

What does the bell-shaped curve in the style-of-parent portion of the model mean? It means that as the maturity level of our child develops along the continuum from immature to mature, the appropriate style of leadership moves accordingly, along the bell-shaped curve, from *telling* (S1) to *selling* (S2) to *participating* (S3) to *delegating* (S4).

Determining Appropriate Style

To determine what initial style is appropriate to use in a given situation, we must first determine the maturity level of our child or children in relation to the specific aspect of their life we wish to influence. Once this maturity level is identified, the appropriate parent style can be determined by drawing a line straight upward from the point on the continuum that identifies our child's maturity level to the bell-shaped curve. The line and curve will intersect in one of the four style quadrants — this tells us the appropriate style to use. Let's look at an example in Figure 3.

Suppose a young mother decides that her son Charlie's maturity is low in the area of keeping his room clean. Charlie definitely does not seem to be willing to keep his room in order and, after examining the situation, his mother realizes that he also does not know how to do a number of the tasks involved in maintaining a clean room, making his bed, straightening his bureau drawers, and so on. Having made that analysis, Charlie's mother places an X on the maturity continuum above the low level of maturity (M1) as shown in Figure 3. Once she has decided to influence Charlie's behavior in this area, Charlie's mother can determine the appropriate initial style to use by drawing a line from the X on the maturity scale to Y on the bell-shaped curve (see Figure 3). Since the intersection occurs in the high directive/low supportive style (S1) quadrant, his mother should use a *telling* style when working with Charlie.

In this example, when we talk about low supportive behavior, we do not mean that Charlie's mother should be unpleasant to Charlie or cross with him. (Notice that the bell-shaped curve in Figure 3 starts part way up in the model.) We are merely suggesting that in supervising Charlie's cleaning of his room, she should spend more time directing Charlie in what to do, and how, when, and where to do it, than in providing support and encouragement. She can increase her support when Charlie begins to demonstrate the ability and motivation to keep his room clean on his own. At that point, a move from "telling" to "selling" would be appropriate.

As you might have noted by now, the four maturity designations — low maturity (M1), low to moderate maturity (M2), moderate to high maturity (M3), and high maturity (M4) — correspond to the four parent style designations: *telling* (S1), *selling* (S2), *participating* (S3), and *delegating* (S4). That is,

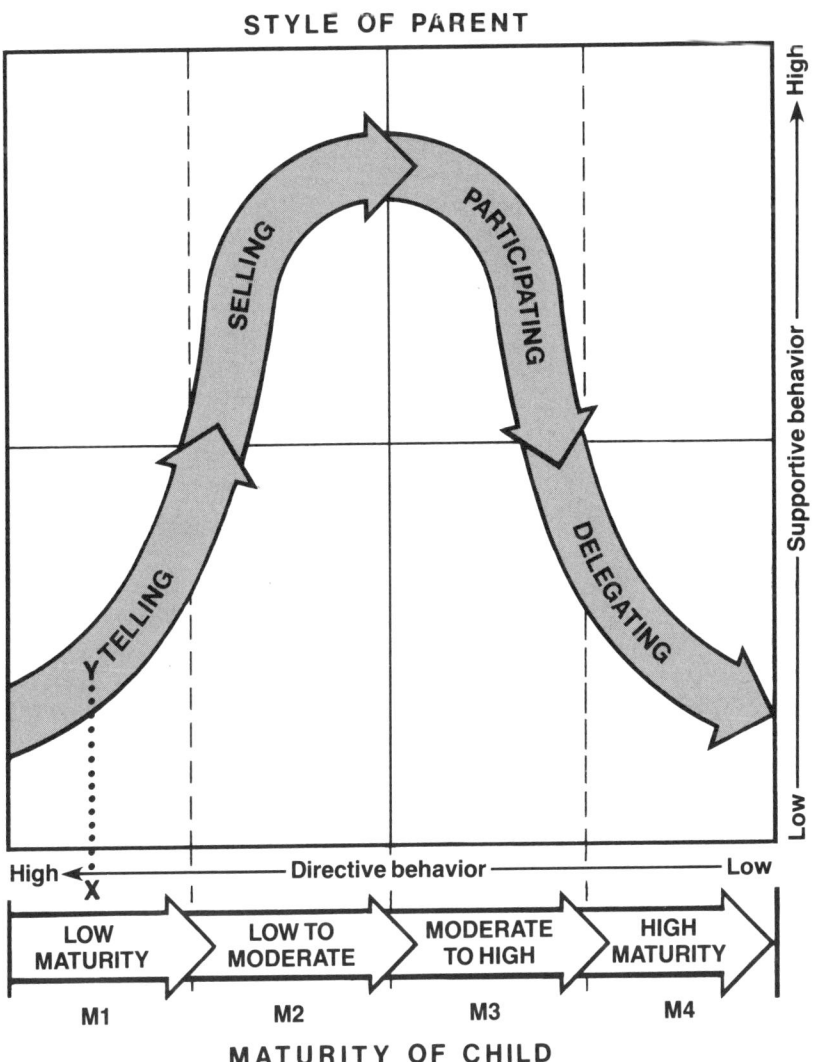

Figure 3. Determining an appropriate leadership style.

low maturity needs a *telling* style, low to moderate maturity needs a *selling* style, and so on. These combinations are shown in Figure 4.

Thus, Situational Leadership suggests that in working with children who are both unwilling and unable (low maturity) to carry out something on their own (M1), a "telling" style (S1) has the highest probability of being effective. A parent using this style tells the child what needs to be done and when, where, and how to do it.

Child — Low Maturity (M1): " *I don't want to put a tie on when we go to Aunt Edith's. Besides, I don't even know how to tie it right. I feel silly in it.*"

Parent — "Telling" (S1): "*Dave, I really want you to wear a tie to Aunt Edith's. Go and get your green tie now and bring it to me so I can show you how to tie it right.*"

In dealing with children who are willing but not able (low to moderate maturity) to take responsibility for doing something on their own (M2), a high directive and high supportive "selling" style (S2) appears to be most appropriate. Children at this maturity level will usually go along with a decision their parents make if they understand why it has to be done and if their parents also offer some help and direction.

Child — Low to Moderate Maturity (M2): "*I'll wear a tie to Aunt Edith's if Dad wants, but I can't understand why I have to. And, besides, I don't know which one to wear or how to put it on right.*"

Parent — "Selling" (S2): "*Dave, this is a dress-up affair at Aunt Edith's, so we'd like you to look nice. Go bring me your green tie and I'll show you how to put it on right. This will make Aunt Edith very happy.*"

In working with children who are able but not willing (moderate to high maturity) to take responsibility for doing something on their own (M3), a supportive, nondirective, "participating" style (S3) has the highest probability of being effective.

MATURITY LEVEL	APPROPRIATE PARENT STYLE
M1 **Low Maturity** Unwilling and unable	**S1** **Telling** High directive and low supportive behavior
M2 **Low to** **Moderate Maturity** Willing but unable	**S2** **Selling** High directive and high supportive behavior
M3 **Moderate To** **High Maturity** Able but unwilling	**S3** **Participating** High supportive and low directive behavior
M4 **High Maturity** Able and willing	**S4** **Delegating** Low supportive and low directive behavior

Figure 4. Parent leadership styles appropriate for the various maturity levels.

Since the child can do the task but lacks enthusiasm or self-confidence, the parents need to open the way for two-way communication and active listening so as to support the child's efforts to use the ability he or she already has.

Child — Moderate to High Maturity (M3)
"I know this is a dress-up affair at Aunt Edith's, and I should wear a tie. I think I know how to fix a tie, but I'll ask Dad to watch, just to make sure I'm doing it right.

Parent — "Participating" (S3)
"Dave, the affair at Aunt Edith's is a dress-up deal, so we'd like you to look nice. Do you have any suggestions? What do you think would be appropriate for you to wear? You really look nice when you are all dressed up. Can I be of any help?"

A low supportive and low directive "delegating" style (S4) has the highest probability of being effective with children who are both willing and able (high maturity) to do something on their own (M4). Even though the parent may still identify the problem, the responsibility for carrying out any plans is given to this mature child.

Child — High Maturity (M4)
"I know that Aunt Edith likes to have me wear a tie when we visit, and I don't mind. I think she's a neat person. Besides, now that I've learned to fix a tie by myself, it's no hassle."

Parent — "Delegating" (S4)
"Dave, we'll be leaving for Aunt Edith's at 4:00. Why don't you try to be dressed and ready at that time?"

Ineffective Parenting Styles

Throughout our discussion we have been suggesting that by using Situational Leadership effectively, we can help our children develop into responsible, healthy, mature individuals. Yet parents often fail at this task. Where do they go wrong?

Frequently, parents keep their children from maturing by using only one of the four styles all the time. Thus, they either control and direct their kids' behavior far too long, or they support and encourage almost any behavior before their children are ready for such responsibility. The consequences of using a single parent style exclusively are predictable.

First, let's look at the parent who uses a high directive "telling" style throughout the developmental years: "As long as you're living in this house, you'll be home by ten o'clock and abide by the rules I've set." Two predictions might be made. The children might pack their bags and leave home at the earliest opportunity. Or, if this does not occur, they might succumb to their parents' authority and become very passive, dependent individuals, always needing someone to tell them what to do and when to do it.

The parent who relies exclusively on a high directive and supportive "selling" style is likely to develop a "Mama's boy" or "Daddy's little girl." Even as adults, such individuals are still psychologically dependent on their parent(s) or some other parent figure to make decisions for them. Since most of their direction, support, and encouragement has been provided by their parent(s), these young people are unable to function on their own.

What happens when parents are unfailingly supportive and never structure or direct any of their children's activities? The result of this "participating" style may be a spoiled brat, a child who has little regard for rules and little consideration for the rights of others.

A "delegating" style which is neither directive nor supportive seems to be characteristic of the very wealthy or very poor. In both cases, the children may become products of their environment rather than products of their parents' style. In the case of the very wealthy, child-rearing responsibility may be delegated to a private school or a "nanny"; in the case of the very poor, children are often left on their own to learn from their siblings or peers how to cope with the day-to-day contingencies of their environment. How these children develop depends more on the quality of their school, nanny, or friends than on the influence of their parents.

What About Consistency?

You might question why it is inappropriate to use the same leadership style all the time. "After all, we've been told that consistency is good." That kind of advice might have been given in the past, but in our terms *consistency* is *not* using the same style all the time. Instead, consistency is using the same style for all similar situations, and varying the style appropriately as the situation changes. Let's assume that a parent has two children, Maria and Sal. Suppose Maria, one afternoon after school, is behaving well at home but Sal is misbehaving. If the parent uses a supportive, "participating" style with both children, that parent would be inconsistent, not consistent. Parents are consistent if they direct their children and discipline them when they are behaving inappropriately, but support and reward them when they are behaving appropriately. Parents are inconsistent, on the other hand, if they smile and respond supportively when their children are "bad" as well as when they are "good".

To be *really* consistent (in our terms) parents must behave the same way in similar situations for all parties concerned. Thus, a consistent parent would not discipline Sal when he misbehaves but not Maria, and vice versa. It is also important for parents to treat their children the same way in similar circumstances even when it is *inconvenient*.

Some parents are consistent only when it is convenient. That leads to problems. For example, suppose Wendy and Walt get upset when their children argue with each other and are willing to "clamp down" on them when it happens. However, there are exceptions to their consistency in this area. If they are rushing off to a dinner party, they will generally not deal with the children's fighting. Or in the supermarket with the kids, they will frequently permit behavior they would normally not let go by, because they are uncomfortable disciplining their children in public. Since children are continually testing the boundaries or limits of their behavior (they want to know what they can and cannot do), Walt and Wendy's kids soon learn that they should not fight with each other except when "Mom and Dad are in a hurry to go out or when we're in a store." Thus, unless parents are willing to be consistent even when it is inconvenient, they may actually be encouraging misbehavior.

Attitude versus Behavior

One of the ideas behind the "old definition" of consistency was the belief that your behavior as a parent *must* be consistent with your attitudes. Therefore, if you love your children, you should also treat them in loving, supportive ways all the time and never engage in restrictive, controlling behavior. And yet, although love is a basic ingredient for effective parents, it may be appropriate for parents to respond in a variety of ways as they face the various family situations. For example, if Scott is young and inexperienced in many ways, the appropriate parent style may be highly directive, with his mother or father directing, controlling, and closely supervising his behavior. While this style may not appear to be a loving style, it might be the one that best meets Scott's need for direction. At the same time, if Carol is emotionally mature and can take responsibility for her own behavior, the appropriate style with her may be a low supportive and low directive one. In this case, her mother or father delegates to Carol the responsibility of controlling and supervising her own behavior. Her parents, while loving her, play a background role, providing support only when necessary. Thus, even though your love for each of your children may be constant, if they behave differently they must be treated differently.

This also holds true for the child who differs in various aspects of his or her life. Take Tom, a high school boy who is very mature in terms of his commitment to football. Even in the summer, he sets his own practice schedule, watches his diet, and gets the proper amount of rest. In this area, his parents do not have to supervise him; he has been playing and practicing football since he was very young and he is willing and able to take responsibility for his own behavior. This is not the case, however, in terms of Tom's school work. In this area, Tom still needs some parental direction and supervision to get his work done. Thus, Tom's parents vary their style according to their son's needs.

Willingness versus "Won'tness"

It is our feeling that during the first three or four years of a child's life, parents have to play the key role in teaching and motivating their children. During those early years, parents spend most of their time teaching and motivating their children to develop new skills — how to eat, walk, speak, stay away from cars, and on and on. In teaching these skills, parents have to learn to use effectively the more directive "telling" and "selling" styles.

As children start school, two things happen which begin to take the load of skill training off parents. First, in our society the skill training of our kids now begins to shift to other individuals and institutions. Reading, writing, and arithmetic now become the job of the schools. Baseball, football, and other team sports become the job of the Little League coaches and recreation directors. Swimming, tennis, golf, horseback riding, and the like are taught by special instructors. When children become teenagers, driving is taught in school, and so on. No longer is the parent the only source of skill training.

Second, children now start to teach each other things they need to know. The peer group plays a significant role in teaching various skills to children.

As a result of these two factors, the skills children need to know are fairly well learned or are being provided by people other than parents by the time kids have started school. Now the emphasis in child rearing begins to shift from the development of skills to purely motivational questions, to dealing with "lures" that compete for our children's time and take them away from what they *should* be doing. The issues now hinge on questions like these: How do we get our kids "turned on" to things? How do we get them to do their homework? Practice the piano? Help around the house? What do we do about TV? As they become older, how do we keep them from getting involved in drinking, drugs, or sex problems? Parents of teenagers are often trying to *stop* their kids from engaging in inappropriate behavior.

If the problem involves our child doing something we don't want the child to do, like "shacking up" with a boyfriend or smoking "pot," ability is not a question. Inappropriate behavior in these cases has to do with abstaining, which is not as much a question of willingness as of "won'tness." It is "won't power" rather than "will power." "Will power" is easy — it means the child wants to do something and is doing it. "Won't power" means the child is willing to say no to something that all his or her friends may be doing, like using drugs. And that's a harder motivational issue, especially with their "friends" saying things like: "Don't knock it if you haven't tried it." "It's the greatest thing since popcorn." "How would your parents know — they're too old!"

To deal with these kinds of pressures and help our children with "won'tness" questions, we must learn to use the more supportive "selling" and "participating" styles. The key to using these styles effectively is beginning early. We want to open up the channels of communication with our children well before they become teenagers. Then when the lure of alcohol, drugs, sex, and other things comes into the picture, our children will be willing to share their anxieties and feelings with us. For that to happen, our children must know that they will not get punished for sharing their feelings and anxieties. This is particularly important since a number of the issues facing young people involve behavior that is not universally "bad" — like sex, which may be more appropriate in other circumstances later in life.

Children need to learn that some things that appear fun on the surface may have ramifications that are difficult to untangle if engaged in before they are well thought out. Our role as parents here is value clarification — not necessarily imposing our values on them but teaching our children how to discriminate for themselves between what they ought to be involved in and what they ought to avoid at various times in their lives.

In teaching values and "won't power" to our children we have to be careful not to place too much emphasis on "won't power" *per se*, or we may create complexes or psychological problems later in life for our children in areas like sex and prevent them from engaging in that aspect of their lives even when it is appropriate. We cannot overemphasize the need to establish open communication with our children early in their lives.

If our relationship with our children is already strained by a lack of communication, the pressures on our teenagers will separate us even more. Then our children will seek support and advice outside the home when they confront questions of values. This is often the case with parents who have left their children alone for some time and then, when a problem occurs (their children do something the parents disapprove of), they are hurt because their children never confided in them earlier when the pressures to do something inappropriate first started. By the time the parents find out about the problem, it is usually already "well down the road." The combination of being hurt, annoyed, and concerned causes them to intervene hard with a "telling" style, when a much earlier "participating" style with active listening might have been appropriate. This "leave alone — zap" approach often drives a wedge between parent and child and creates resentment on both sides.

In essence, if we parents help our children mature in healthy ways over time, the movement is from directing, controlling, and supervising the behavior of our children to being available for support, active listening, and advice in a way that helps them sort out their values and life plans. Our hope is that eventually our children will behave in mature, responsible ways no matter whether we are around or not.

Supervising What Children Learn Outside the Home

Reverend Jesse Jackson, the Chicago minister who is a great believer in parent involvement in education, once gave a powerful talk[3] in which he told how he had gone to a racetrack one day to observe what people did at such an establishment. He said he was interested to observe the differences in the behavior of the people waiting in line to bet at the $100 window and the people at the $2 window.

There were very few people at the $100 window and those who were there were quiet and very serious as they studied their programs and decided on their bet. At the $2 window there were many more people, but quiet and serious they were not. In fact, all they seemed to be doing was eating hot dogs, drinking beer, and talking loudly. Most of them didn't seem to know which horse they were going to bet on until they got up to the window. When the race was about to start, those at the $100 window rushed to their seats and focused their binoculars on the horses as they entered the starting gate. They looked at the horses, the jockeys, and the track with much interest. The people at the $2 window, however, didn't seem to move even when the race started. They still hung around the $2 window, eating hot dogs and drinking beer. A number of them by now had lost their tickets and couldn't recall which horse they had bet on.

As the race progressed the people from the $100 window continued carefully to observe and monitor what was happening in the race, while the people at the $2 window continued to mill around, eating hot dogs, drinking beer, and talking loudly, even as the horses were racing for the finish line. By that time they were beginning to regroup in line to place their new bet on "who knows?"

Reverend Jackson suggested that many of our parents today are at the $2 window when it comes to the education of their children. They send them off to school in the morning and then just sit around the house eating hot dogs, drinking beer, and talking loudly. He thinks it's about time we as parents got up to the $100 window when it comes to the education of our children and studied and monitored what's happening to them in this important aspect of their life.

Reverend Jackson's point is a very important one, especially when we consider the number of aspects of a child's life we delegate to the school, other individuals, and other groups. If our children are to develop into independent, self-motivated individuals in these areas, the people involved in their training must know how to develop skills and motivation. We cannot turn our backs on what is happening to our children and sit home "eating hot dogs, drinking beer, and talking loudly." If we do, our child could be having a poor learning experience that might take years to overcome. That would be abdication, not delegation. Let's look at the situation of a father who intervened in his child's school, to see what we are talking about.

The father was familiar with Situational Leadership and was able to use the concept in deciding what needed to be done when he learned that his son Matt was tested as two years ahead of his fourth-grade class in math, but two years behind in reading.

When the father met with Matt's teacher he asked, "How do you treat Matt differently during math period versus reading?" The teacher said, "We belong to a special math program. Each child has his or her own math folder in one of the files on the far wall. When it's math period, the kids get up and go to the files and pull out their math folders, return to their desks, and start doing math problems where they left off last class."

"How's that approach working with Matt in math?" the father asked.

"Really well," said the teacher. "He's one of my best math students."

"What do the kids do during reading period?" asked Matt's father.

The reply was much the same. Each child has his or her own reading folder in one of the files on the near wall. When it's reading period, the kids get up and go to the files and pull out their reading folders, return to their desks, and resume reading where they left off last class."

"How's that approach working with Matt in reading?" asked Matt's father.

"Not very well," said the teacher. "As you know, Matt is doing very poorly in reading."

"Did you ever think that sometimes you have to use a different teaching style with the same kid on a different subject?" inquired Matt's father.

He asked this question because it became apparent that the teacher was using the same "delegating" style with Matt in reading as she was using in math. In analyzing Matt's maturity level in math, we can see that he was both willing and able (high maturity) to take responsibility for directing his own behavior in this subject area. In fact, Matt was confused about the difference between work and play in math, as he really thought it was all fun. For example, he continually asked his parents to give him math problems to solve when they were riding in the car on trips. Using Situational Leadership, it is clear why the "delegating" style that was being used with Matt in math was working.

In terms of reading, Matt's maturity level was a different story. To him reading was a "drag" — he didn't seem to be willing or able to direct his own learning in reading (low maturity — M1). As a result, the "delegating" style the teacher was using in reading was a mismatch for his low level of maturity. Realizing that Matt really needed a "telling" style of leadership, his father told the teacher that they (Matt's parents) would work closely with Matt at home and asked if she could do the same at school. In fact, he suggested that it might be helpful for a while if the teacher walked over to Matt at the beginning of reading, picked out his folder with him, gave him a specific assignment and then checked on him periodically during reading period.

With the parents and the teacher changing to a more directive, "telling" style with Matt in reading, it didn't take long for his reading to improve. At the same time his teacher began to realize that her supportive, nondirective style was not good for all the kids all the time, and that it was sometimes helpful to use other approaches to teaching.

We've told you about Matt's reading problem for two reasons. First, we wanted to emphasize our belief that not only should different leadership styles be used in different situations, but the overuse of any one style can lead to problems. Second, while parents might delegate the teaching of some skills to specialists in the community, they should be aware of their children's progress in these areas and feel free to intervene if needed.

Changing Leadership Style Appropriately

"How do we know when it's time to change styles?" many parents ask. One indicator we can use in determining when and to what degree we should shift our style is our children's performance or behavior. How well are our children performing in their present activities? If performance is improving, it would be appropriate to shift our style to the right on the bell-shaped curve (see Figure 2), that is, from "telling" to "selling" or "selling" to "participating," and so on. This would indicate that maturity is increasing. If, on the other hand, performance and behavior are on the decline, it gives us a clue that we may need to shift our leader behavior to the left along the bell-shaped curve in the Situational Leadership model. In the next four chapters we discuss specifically how these processes work.

3 · *Growing Winners*

If we, as parents, are to play a role in helping our children become "winners," it will be useful to understand first how we can use Situational Leadership as a framework for developing the independence and maturity of our children over a period of time.

We think this developmental aspect of Situational Leadership is vital. Without it, some parents might misuse the model to justify the use of almost any behavior they care to try. Since the theory suggests that there is no "best" leadership style, the use of any style could be explained simply by saying, "My child is at such and such a maturity level." Our point is that while close supervision and direction might be necessary initially when working with children who have had little experience in directing their own behavior, this style is only a first step. In fact, parents should try gradually to work themselves out of their traditional job of directing, controlling, and supervising the behavior of their children as the children learn to assume more and more responsibility themselves.

What does this mean for us as parents? This means that if we are using a leadership style with a high probability of success for a given level of maturity (as we talked about in Chapter 2), this perhaps is not enough. While we may have well-behaved children, our responsibilities do not stop here.

One of the ways to keep our leadership style current is to be alert to changes in our children's behavior. As we see a child become more responsible in a given area, consider changing our style to the right on the curve in the Situational

Leadership model — that is, from "telling" to "selling" and so on, as illustrated in Figure 1. For example, suppose we have been directing and closely supervising ("telling") our son while he clips the hedges and we now notice that he seems to be really catching on. At this point we might want to consider a shift to "selling," where we still maintain some supervision of our child in this area but are willing to answer questions and clarify what has to be done. If we were already using a "selling" style with our child, we might want to shift to a "participating" style, where we are supportive of his efforts and provide opportunities for him to make suggestions but provide little direction or supervision. Finally, if we were using a "participating" style for a period of time and the job is being handled well with little direction, we might now want to let him take care of the hedge clipping on his own.

It would be great if parents only had to respond to increased maturity from their children, but, as we all know, parents must also respond to their children when they seem to be showing less responsibility in a given area. We will discuss how to handle decreasing maturity in Chapter 5, "Turning It Around."

What we have been describing in this example is our responses to progress that occurs in the behavior of our child. While that is an important aspect of child rearing, we feel that the role of a parent involves more than just reacting to changes in child maturity. This is particularly true if we assume that one of the responsibilities of parents is to help children grow and develop into mature, responsible, and self-motivated adults. If we would like to be a catalyst to such growth, the process we call the "developmental cycle" may be helpful.

The Developmental Cycle

We feel the role we as parents play in developing the maturity of our children is extremely important. Too often we blame everyone else (i.e., the school, friends, neighborhoods) for the way our children behave, and yet, if we accept our role as

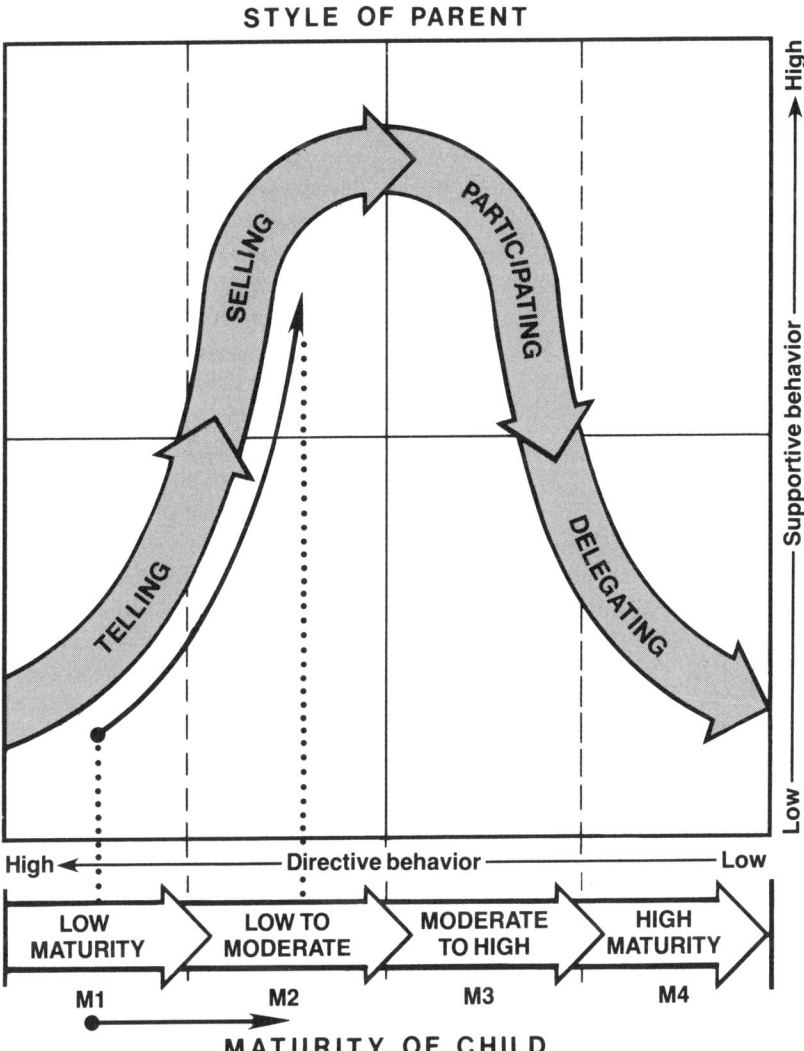

Figure 1. When the maturity level of a child increases in a particular area, the style of the parent should shift to the right along the curve in the Situational Leadership model.

parents we must also accept the responsibility of being a major influencer of our children's behavior. Parents are involved in the developmental cycle any time they attempt to increase the present maturity level of their children in some aspect of their lives. In other words, the developmental cycle is a growth cycle.

What Do We Want to Influence?

Perhaps the first question to ask ourselves is: "What areas of my child's life do I want to influence?" Parents of a young baby might want to influence when the child eats, goes to sleep, and so on. As the child gets older, the areas of life a parent might want to influence usually get more complicated. A parent then might want to influence the child's manners, school work, respect for elders, responsibility, and the like.

Once we have identified the areas of our child's life we want to influence, we must specify clearly what consitutes good behavior in each area, so that both we and our child know when the child's behavior is approaching what is desired. What does eating well mean? Everything is cleaned off the plate, or at least some of everything. What does having good manners mean, or doing a good job on homework? Parents have to specify what good behavior *looks like*. Just telling a child, "I want you to keep your room clean," is not as helpful as saying, "I want you to keep your room clean. What I mean by a 'clean room' is that your bed is made, your toys and everything are picked up off the floor, your wastepaper basket is emptied, and all your bureau drawers are neat." Even that final statement might need further explanation. While a child might have no trouble understanding what an emptied wastepaper basket looks like, a "neat" bureau drawer could be more open to debate. For you and the child to know how well the child is doing, what "good" behavior looks like has to be clearly specified.

If two parents are involved in child rearing, it's important that they agree on what "good" behavior means in a particular area. If one parent says the child's room is neat and the other parent says it's a mess, then they have not sufficiently specified the behavior they want to influence. Parents cannot change or develop their child's behavior in something that is unclear.

How is Our Child Doing Now?

Before beginning the developmental cycle with a child in a particular area, we must agree on how well our child is doing right now. In other words, what is the child's maturity level at this moment in time? How able is the child to take responsibility for his or her own behavior in this area? How willing or motivated is the child? As we discussed earlier, maturity is not a global concept. That is, children are not mature or immature in any total sense. How can we know what our child's maturity level is in a particular area?

Determining Maturity

In assessing the maturity level of our child in a particular area, we will have to make judgments about his or her ability and motivation. Where do we get information to make such judgments? We can either *ask* our children or *observe* their behavior.

We could ask our children such questions as, "How good do you think you are at doing such and such?" "How do you feel about doing it?" "Are you excited and enthusiastic about it or not?" Obviously, with very young children, asking for their assessment of their own maturity level isn't possible. However, we may be surprised how early children will share that kind of information. Phil and Jane learned that when they used to ask their two-year-old daughter, Lee, to do something. Often she would reply, "I can't want to!" When translated, what Lee was really saying (in our terms) is, "I'm both unable and unwilling to do what you want me to do." If Lee's parents still wanted her to do it, they soon learned they had to direct and closely supervise her behavior in this area ("telling"). As children get older they can play an even more significant role in analyzing their own maturity level.

You might be wondering whether children will always tell their parents the truth, or will they just tell them what is necessary to keep the parents "off their backs." If we doubt what our children tell us about their ability or willingness to do something, we can check out their opinion by observing their behavior. Ability can be determined by examining past performance. Has our child done well in this area before, or has his or her performance been poor or nonexistent? Does our child have the necessary knowledge to perform well in this area, or does he or she not know how to do what needs to be done?

Willingness can be determined by watching our child's behavior in a particular area. What is our child's interest level? Does he or she seem enthusiastic, or energyless and uninterested? What is the child's commitment to this area? Does he or she appear to enjoy doing things in this area, or merely anxious to get it over with? Is our child self-confident and secure in this area, or does he or she lack confidence and feel insecure?

Remember, children can be at any of four levels of maturity in each area of their life. A child's maturity level gives us a good clue as to how to begin any further development of the child. If we want to influence one of our children in an area where that child is both unable and unwilling (low maturity), we must begin the developmental cycle by directing, controlling, and closely supervising ("telling") his or her behavior. If, however, our child is willing (motivated) to do something but not able to do it (low to moderate maturity), we must begin the cycle by both directing and supporting ("selling") the desired behavior. If our child is able to do something on his or her own but is unwilling to do it (moderate to high maturity), we are faced with a motivational problem. A child's reluctance to do what he or she is able to do is often the result of insecurity or lack of confidence. In this case, the parent should begin the developmental cycle by using a supportive style ("participating") to help the child to become secure enough to be able to do what he or she already knows how to do. And, finally, if one of our children is both able and willing to direct his or her own behavior (high maturity), we can merely delegate responsibility to the child and know the child will behave well. When that occurs, there is no need for beginning the developmental cycle. Our child is already mature in that area.

To better understand how the developmental cycle works, let's look at the case of a mother who decides to develop her child in an area where the child is at a low maturity level. Suppose the mother has determined that the maturity of her daughter Diana is low (M1) in the area of doing the dishes after dinner. She decides to influence Diana's behavior in this area. As we discussed in Chapter 2, if Diana's mother knows that Diana's maturity level is low — Diana is unable and unwilling to take responsibility (M1) for washing the dishes after dinner — then she should realize that she must start the developmental cycle by using a directive "telling" style (S1). What would a "telling" style look like in this situation?

It would involve several things for Diana's mother. First, she would have to tell Diana exactly what is involved in washing the dishes — clearing off the table, scraping the leftover food into the garbage can, rinsing the dishes off, and so on. Second, she would begin to show Diana how to do each of the tasks involved. Thus, "telling" in a teaching situation involves "show and tell"; Diana must be told what to do and then shown how to do it. While this "telling" style is high on direction and low on support, this does not mean that Diana's mother is not being friendly to her. Low supportive behavior in this situation merely means that her mother is not patting Diana on the back before she has earned it. Until then, Diana's mother emphasizes explaining the what, when, where, and hows of the job.

Taking Risks

If Diana's mother uses a "telling" style in this situation, the dishes will probably be done fairly well, since she is working closely with Diana. But if she assumes that one of the child-rearing responsibilities of a parent is to help children grow and develop in maturity and independence, then she has to be willing to take a risk. This means she should begin to permit Diana to take some responsibility on her own, without as much direction and supervision from her parents. This is particularly true if Diana has not assumed much responsibility in the past for doing the dishes. While taking a risk is a reality in the developmental cycle, parents have to keep the degree of risk reasonable. It should not be too high. In our example, Diana's mother is risking a few broken dishes. It would be wise, then, to start Diana off on old dishes, or even plastic dishes, rather than grandma's priceless bone china. So it's not a question of whether to take a risk or not; it's a matter of taking a calculated risk.

Learning "A Little Bit at a Time"[1]

If a parent asks a child to do something he or she has never been taught to do and expects good performance the first time, even though no help is offered the child, the parent has set the child up for failure and punishment. This begins the widely used "tell, leave alone, and then 'zap'" approach to child rearing. The parent tells the child what to do (without bothering to find out if the child knows how to do it), leaves the child alone (expecting immediate results), and then yells at and punishes the child when the desired behavior does not follow.

If Diana's mother used this approach with her daughter, the events might look something like this. The mother might assume that at ten years of age a child should be able to do the dishes by herself. So, one night when she has company, she asks Diana to help out by doing the dishes for her while she entertains her friends. Not bothering to analyze whether Diana is willing or able to do the dishes on her own, her mother gives the order and then goes into the living room to visit with her friends. When she comes back into the kitchen to get more coffee a half hour later, rather than finding the dishes done, she finds a worse mess than when she left, including some of her best dishes broken. Diana's mother completely "blows her cool," screams and yells at Diana, spanks her, and sends her to her room.

Parents should remember that no one, including themselves, learns how to do anything all at once. We learn a little bit at a time. As a result, if a parent wants a child to do something completely new, the parent should reward the slightest progress the child makes in the desired direction. This is a process known as *positive reinforcement* of small accomplishments on the way to a final goal (new learning).

Many parents use this process already without really being aware of it. For example, how do you think we teach a child to walk? Imagine if we stood a child up and said, "Walk," and then when he fell down we spanked him for not walking. Sound ridiculous? Of course. But it's not really any different than the mother's anger with Diana. A child spanked for falling down will soon not try to walk, since he knows this leads to punishment. At this point he's not even sure what his legs are for. Therefore parents usually first teach a child how to stand up. If the child stays up even for a second or two, his parents get excited and hug and kiss him, call his grandmother, and the like. Next, when the child can stand and hold onto a table, his parents again hug and kiss him. The same happens when he takes his first step, even if he falls down. Whether or not his parents know it, they are positively rewarding the child for small accomplishments as he moves closer and closer to the desired behavior — walking.

In terms of our Situational Leadership model, in order for us to help our child mature — get our child to take more and more responsibility — we must first tell and show our child what to do (directive behavior); second, give *some* responsibility to the child (not too much or failure might result); and third, reward as soon as possible any behavior in the desired direction (supportive behavior). This process should continue as our child's behavior more and more closely approaches our expectations of appropriate behavior. What would supportive behavior look like in this situation?

Supportive behavior would involve "patting the child on the head," providing "positive strokes" and reinforcement. Positive reinforcement or strokes are anything that is desired or needed by the child whose behavior is being reinforced. While directive behavior precedes the desired behavior, supportive behavior or positive reinforcement follows the desired behavior and increases the likelihood of it reoccurring.

It's important to remember that reinforcement must immediately follow any behavior in the desired direction. Reinforcement at a later time will be of less help in getting our children to do something they've never done before on their own.

To better understand how this concept of learning a little

bit at a time works in terms of Situational Leadership, let's consider another example. Suppose the Washingtons want to begin to develop the maturity level of their son and daughter in the area of taking care of themselves without a babysitter. Since their children have no past experience in this area — i.e., they are at the lowest maturity level — the first step in the developmental cycle would be for the Washingtons to tell the children they are going next door for a while and explain to them what they can or cannot do while they are gone. In other words, they should be very directive with the children, using a "telling" style, as illustrated by Point A in Figure 2. When they feel the children understand what is expected of them, the Washingtons could begin to move their style from Point A to a more supportive and less directive style (Point C in Figure 2) by decreasing their directive behavior (Step 2) to Point B. This is the risky step, since they will be leaving the children alone for a short while. If when they return in fifteen or twenty minutes they find the children playing well together and everything in order, it is then appropriate for the Washingtons to engage in Step 3 — positively reinforcing their kids' good behavior by being more supportive of them (Point C), as shown in Figure 2. This might mean praising the children, buying them ice cream cones, or doing something else they would enjoy.

Remember, it's not a good idea to turn over too much responsibility too rapidly. This is a common error many parents make. If our child can't handle it, as was discussed earlier, we may be setting him or her up for failure and frustration. Children who experience these feelings often are reluctant to try anything on their own again in the near future. In our example, the Washingtons may start off appropriately by telling their children what they expect of them, but then be gone visiting friends down the street for several hours. They are too far away for too long a time to be aware of their children's behavior. As we have suggested, this abrupt movement from "telling" to "delegating" often sets the children up for failure and punishment, as it assumes that telling is learning. Later, when the Washingtons return home and find "all hell has broken loose," they are likely to scold their kids by saying

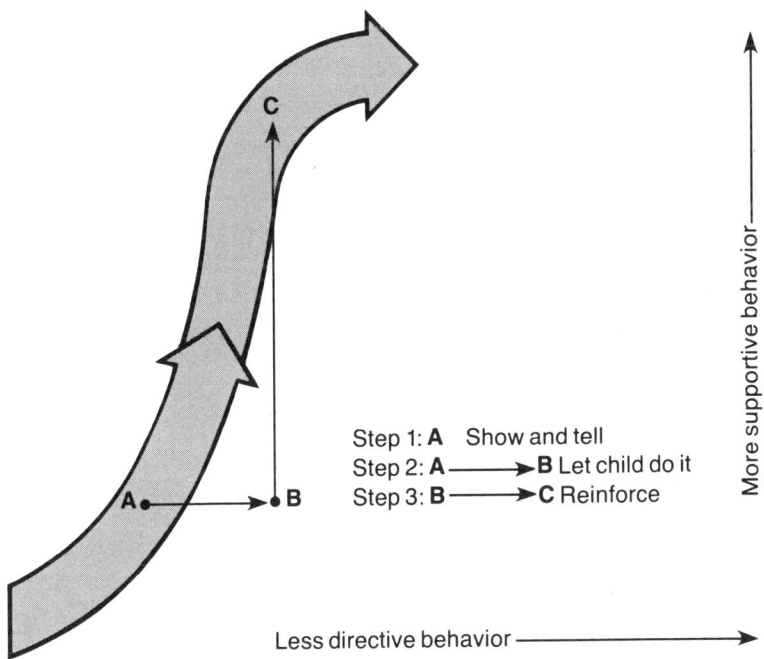

Figure 2. The three steps of the developmental cycle.

something like, "What's the matter with you kids? We told you not to fight and make a mess and look what we find. We're really mad at you both. There will be no T.V. tonight and you will go to bed early."

In addition to not turning over too much responsibility too rapidly, parents should be warned not to increase supportive behavior without first getting the desired behavior. That is why the Washingtons in our example do not move immediately from Point A to Point C along the curved line in Figure 2. If they moved from Point A to Point C without some evidence that their children could take care of themselves for a short while at Point B, the children might think their parents were not serious about them not fighting in their absence or that their parents were just "old softies." It would be like giving our son $6.00 on Thursday to cut the grass sometime during the coming weekend. What do you think our chances are of getting our son to cut the lawn on the weekend, much less doing a good job, when the reward is already in his pocket? Be careful of giving a reward before it is earned. Thus, parents should develop the maturity of their children slowly, using less directive behavior and more supportive behavior as they mature and become more willing and able to take responsibility. When children are inexperienced in some area, parents must not expect drastic changes overnight.

If the Washingtons find that their children are unable to handle themselves alone when their parents are next door for a short while (when they decrease their directive behavior), they might have to return to a more appropriate level of direction. For example, they might first give their children responsibility for taking care of themselves when their parents are working in the backyard or basement. If the children now behave well at that level of supervision, the Washingtons can increase their supportive behavior. Although this level of supportive behavior would be less than if they had behaved well the first time, it matches the amount of responsibility their children, at that time, are able to assume.

As shown in Figure 3, this three-step process (telling and showing, cutting back direction and supervision, and then increasing supportive behavior to reward positive performance if the children respond well to additional responsibility) tends to continue in small steps until the children are assuming moderate levels of responsibility. This continual decreasing of direction does not mean that there is less direction but that the direction is now being provided internally by the children (self-direction) rather than externally by their parents.

An interesting thing occurs in the developmental cycle when the high point of the curved line in the model is reached. This is where the line crosses the mean or average of directive behavior in the upper portion of the model, as well as the mean maturity in the lower portion of the model. Past this point, parents who are appropriately using "participating" or "delegating" leadership styles (S3 or S4) are interacting with children of *moderate* to *high* levels of maturity (M3 to M4). At that

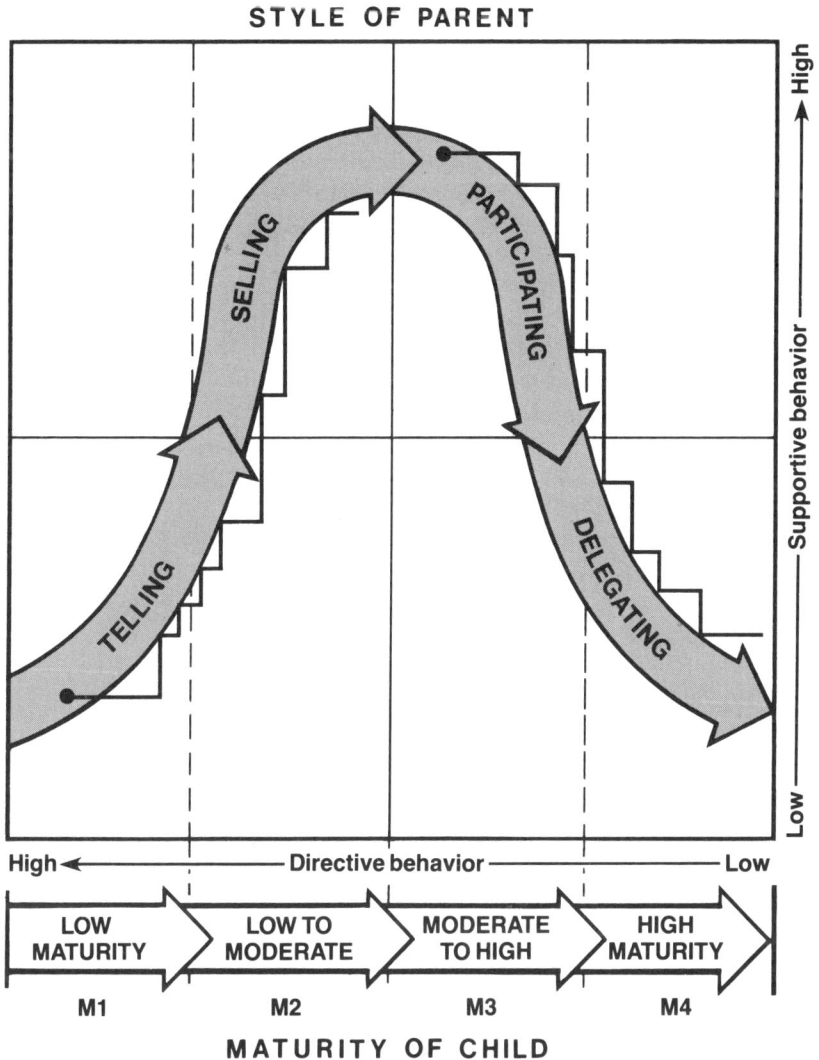

Figure 3. Developmental cycle as children mature over time.

time the process changes and becomes one of the parents not only reducing supervision, but also, when the children can handle their responsibility, cutting back on the amount of supportive behavior. Now the children are not only able to direct their own behavior but they can also provide much of their own "head patting." For example, at a high maturity level the Washingtons would be able to go to a restaurant across town for the evening, and the children would take care of themselves without their parents getting after them or making a big fuss. Taking care of themselves when their parents are out is now rewarding to the children in and of itself. This continuation of the bit by bit learning process is also illustrated in Figure 3.

You might now be asking, "If we reduce the amount of support we give our children, doesn't this show we lack confidence and trust in them?" If we think about it for a moment, we'll realize the answer is no. When we are able to reduce the amount of direction and support we give our child, this indicates that there is, in fact, *more* mutual trust and confidence. Now we don't have to engage in as much supportive behavior to prove it. We are now more dependent on personal power than on position power — trust and commitment from our child rather than on our control over rewards, punishments, and sanctions.

Let's take this a step further. It's important to recognize that, as children mature, their motives and needs are likely to change. For example, children who are not yet able to take responsibility tend to view increased support and help as positive reinforcement. In fact, if their parents left them too much on their own, their fears, anxieties, and insecurities would no doubt be reinforced. As a result, low supportive behavior at this time could be perceived as a punishment rather than a reward. On the other hand, as a child moves to higher levels of maturity, he or she does not require as much "head patting" or as many "positive strokes." This suggests that the child is not only more mature in terms of ability in this area, but also in terms of motivation. The child is more self-confident and has a higher need for autonomy.

When this process begins, one way we can demonstrate confidence and trust in our children is to leave them more and more on their own. You have probably sensed the embarrassment and frustration of some kids when their parents are too supportive of them in front of others ("You really did a good job on the lawn today, Johnny. I'm proud of you."). Thus, while supportive behavior from the parent tends to be positive reinforcement when children are dependent, too much support for children at high levels of maturity is not viewed as a reward. In fact, it can be interpreted by these mature children as a lack of confidence and trust on the part of their parents.

Time and the Developmental Cycle

There is no timetable parents can consult to determine the time necessary to mature children in a particular area. In a simple task, parents may take a child through the total cycle from low maturity to high maturity in a matter of minutes. For example, suppose Alex, a five-year-old boy, has never attempted to tie his own shoes, and his dad thinks that it's about time he learn. Since it's a brand new task for Alex, his father will have to start off being very directive. He will explain what to do, how to do it, when to do it, and where to do it. In essence, Alex's father must move into the early stages of coaching and counseling by providing Alex with "hands-on experience."

As Alex begins to show the ability to do some of those functions, his dad will reduce the amount of telling behavior and increase to some extent supportive behavior. ("That's fine! Good! You're getting it!") And perhaps in a matter of minutes Alex's father may change from a highly directive style to just being close by, where he can provide a moderate amount of direction, as well as high levels of both verbal and nonverbal support and help. In another few minutes Alex's dad may leave Alex to practice on his own while staying close enough to come to the rescue if Alex falters. Thus, in a matter of ten to fifteen minutes, Alex's father has taken Alex in shoe-tying from "telling" through "selling" and "participating" to almost complete delegation (style 4) of that function to Alex. This does *not* mean that "delegating" is always the best style to use with Alex. It just means that in this specific task (shoe-tying) it is the most appropriate one.

Of course, in a more difficult aspect of a child's life, like getting homework done, parents may be doing very well to move a child from a low maturity level to a moderate maturity level over a period of months. Or they may discover that one of their children will "hit the books" much more readily and rapidly than the other children in the family. Even within the general area of homework, children may vary in their ability and motivation from subject to subject, and thus it may take parents different amounts of time to move their children toward self-direction in various subjects.

In sum, the amount of time it takes for a child to mature in a certain area depends on the complexity of the specific responsibility and the willingness and ability of the child.

Are Parents Always in Charge of the Developmental Cycle?

In attempting to influence our children, we can potentially control two things: (1) what they are to do, and (2) what reward or reinforcement they will receive for doing it. This means we can control the amount of direction (what to do) and support (the reinforcement for doing) *we* provide for our children. But will we alone always be in control of the developmental cycle? What about our kids? Won't they have some involvement?

Parent after parent tells us that their chief dilemma is getting their children to do things they (the parents) have decided the children should do. What they aren't realizing is that, although parent domination of the developmental process may be appropriate for working with children at low levels of maturity, the developmental cycle should become more and more of a collaborative process as children mature. In fact, if parents move a child through the entire developmental process from "telling" to "delegating," the process should move (as Lloyd Homme[2] suggests) from parental domination to collaboration between parent and child to self-management for the child as the child demonstrates both willingness and ability to direct his or her own behavior in a responsible manner.

When a parent is appropriately using a "telling" style with an immature child, the parent tells the child what to do and what he or she will get (the reinforcement) for doing it. If the child accepts the parent's direction and carries out the desired behavior, the parent delivers the reward.

Parent	Child
If you stop fighting with your brother, you can watch TV tonight.	*Okay, Mom.*

Notice that the parent in this example makes a positive contract[3] with the child. Often, however, the approach is very different. Most parents tend to use a negative approach which sounds something like, "If you don't do such and such, you will get punished." The above exchange, for example, would read, "If you don't stop fighting with your brother, you will have to go to bed early tonight." Making positive contracts with children not only makes the family atmosphere more pleasant, it also makes more sense to follow good behavior with a reward rather than no punishment. It can turn nagging parents into helpful parents. It also can make parents aware that they should reward their children for mature behavior and not just when they feel like it, as so many parents do.

If the child behaves well under a "telling" style, the parent may appropriately move to a "selling" style. With a "selling" style the parent retains most of the control of determining what the child is to do but lets the child play a key role in deciding what reinforcement will be given if the child behaves well.

Parent
Nancy, I think you ought to start taking guitar lessons. It's a good instrument for you to learn. If you do a good job on lessons until Thanksgiving, what special treat would you like to get yourself?

Child
I'd love to get a new dress for Christmas.

If the child behaves well under "selling," the parent may appropriately move to a style somewhere between "selling" and "participating" in which the parent and child jointly decide both what the child is to do and the reinforcement.

Parent

Shawn, I could use a hand around the house on Saturday. Do you think you could help me out?

Child

I think so, Dad. What did you have in mind for me to do?

Parent

No job in particular, but how about cutting the lawn and cleaning out the garage?

Child

That would be okay. If I take care of those jobs, could I use the car on Saturday night?

Parent

Sure. That would be fine.

Child

It's a deal!

If the child behaves well under this joint decision-making style, the parent may appropriately move to a "participating" style. With this supportive style, the child usually has full control over what is to be done and shares joint control with the parent over the reinforcement to be given.

Child

Mom, I'd like to get all A's and B's this semester.

Parent

That sounds great to me!

Child

If I get all A's and B's, what can I get special to celebrate?

Parent

I don't know. How about a series of tennis lessons from the pro at the park?

Child

That would be great! He's supposed to be very good.

Parent

It's a deal then. If you get those good grades, we'll pay for your tennis lessons.

And finally, if a child behaves well under a "participating" style, the parent may appropriately decide to shift to a "delegating" style. With a "delegating" style, what the child is to do and the reinforcement to be received are determined by the child. In this situation, the child decides to do something, does it, and then delivers self-reinforcement.

Parent

I understand drinking is getting to be a real problem at school, Jesse.

Child

I think it has. But I've decided not to drink like some of the kids are doing. I've tried it and it just doesn't make me feel good. It makes us do stupid things, too.

Parent

I'll leave that up to you, Jesse. You're responsible enough now to decide what's right for you.

As Figure 4 suggests, in moving through the developmental cycle a parent moves from *parent control* ("telling") of what a child is to do and the reward the child will get for doing it to *partial control by children* ("selling") to *equal control* ("selling" and "participating") to *partial control by parent* ("participating") to *child control* ("delegating").

Positive Reinforcement: The Key to Growing Winners

The key to developing the maturity of our children is to follow any progress our child makes toward a desirable behavior with positive reinforcement — the sooner the better. Behavior is influenced by its immediate consequences, and if a certain behavior is followed rapidly by positive reinforcement, the likelihood of our child engaging in that behavior again will be increased. Let's look at that idea a bit more closely.

Individualizing Reinforcement

When applying positive reinforcement, it helps to remember that *reinforcement depends on the child.* What is reinforcing to one child may not be reinforcing to another. Praise may motivate some children to behave better; for others, a new bike or toy might be the most rewarding thing. What "turns on" one child may not "turn on" another.

An example might be helpful. Suppose our child keeps his room sloppy and we want to get him to start taking care of it. Now, if he knows how to keep his room neat (he has the ability to do it), then we must try to find a reinforcer that would motivate him to engage in the behavior we want. This happened in a family we know. Early one September the parents told their son, David, that if he started to take care of his room, he probably would find a new bicycle under the Christmas tree. Since David wanted a bike so badly "he could taste it," there was an immediate change in his behavior. He began to keep his room clean enough to pass a military inspection.

Since his parents realized that Christmas was a long time to wait for a reinforcement, they began to go "shopping for"

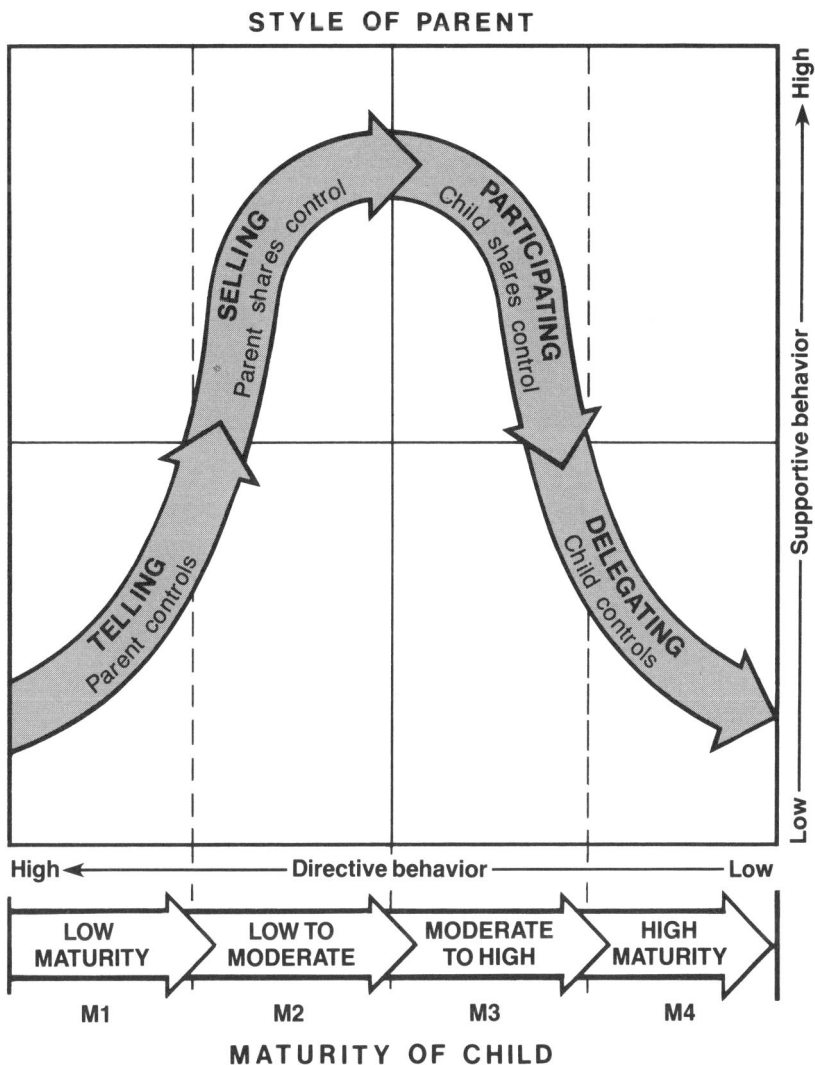

Figure 4. Parental control changes as the maturity of the child increases.

a bike with him when he started to show progress on his room. They took David to look at all kinds of bikes and accessories, like lights, horns, and so on. The result was that David kept his room very clean and, sure enough, a new bicycle — just the one he wanted — was waiting for him under the tree.

Now a year or so later his younger brother, Michael, began having trouble with his room. So his parents, remembering what had worked for David, said in September, "Michael, if you start taking care of your room, a new bicycle might be waiting for you under the Christmas tree." Then the parents waited for the behavior change, but none followed. They tried a new tack: "Michael, if you don't start shaping up that room of yours you can forget about that bike at Christmas." Finally, after about a month of no progress on his room and continued threats of no bike, Michael sat his parents down one night and told them, "I really don't want a bike . . . but a dog — that would be great!"

It also helps to remember that the same child at different times will be motivated by different things, depending on his or her present needs. So, while at one time a child might respond to a bike as a reinforcer, at another time that same child might instead be eager merely for more praise and recognition. Thus, there is a danger in overgeneralizing; each child is likely to experience very different needs at different times. We will go into this in detail in the next chapter, "What's Good for the Goose May Not Be Good for the Gander."

How Often Should We Reinforce a Child's Behavior?

Once our child is engaging in a new behavior, how can we make sure he or she will not revert back to old behavior after a while. The key is in scheduling reinforcement in an effective way.

When our child is first learning to do something completely new, we must reinforce *every behavior* that is in the direction of the desired behavior (remember "Learning a Little Bit at a Time"). This continuous reinforcement will help our child learn the desired behavior quickly. Once the child has learned the new behavior, however, you should switch to periodic rather than continual reinforcement. This periodic reinforcement (or intermittent reinforcement as it is called by psychologists) can be either completely random or scheduled according to a prescribed number of occurrences of the desired behavior or a particular interval of elapsed time. With continuous reinforcement, the child learns the new behavior quickly; but if the environment for that individual changes to one of non-reinforcement, a reverting back to old behavior can be expected to take place relatively soon. With periodic reinforcement, regression is much slower, because the child has become accustomed to going for periods of time without any reinforcement. Thus, for fast learning, continuous reinforcement is our best bet. But once our child has learned the new pattern, a switch to periodic reinforcement should ensure a long-lasting change.

Consider the case of Carlos, a manufacturer's sales representative whose job has recently changed. He will soon be travelling quite a lot. If he wants his six-year-old son, Manuel, to behave well and help his mom out while he is gone, Manuel's father could help that happen. When he first begins to travel, he could tell Manuel that he would bring him a present when he returned if his mom gave him a "good report" — that is, if she said he behaved and was helpful. If Manuel was excited about getting a present and his father had one for him after every one of his early trips when Manuel got a "good report," Manuel would probably try hard to behave well and be helpful when his father was gone.

Now, Manuel's father probably does not want to have to bring home a present every time he goes on a trip and, besides, if he did and then forgot once, Manuel might think the present deal was over and revert back to earlier behavior. So, as soon as Manuel starts to behave consistently well when his father is gone, Carlos should begin to bring a present home only periodically. Gradually he might bring a present home less and less. He wants Manuel to continue to behave well when he is gone, but must move away from continuous reinforcement to periodic reinforcement to help Manuel begin to *internalize* good behavior.

How does this fit into Situational Leadership? In the early stages of a developmental cycle, whenever a parent delegates some responsibility to a child at a low level of maturity and that child performs well, the parent should provide continuous (100 percent) reinforcement. That is, every time the parent cuts back on directive behavior and the child responds well, the parent should immediately increase supportive behavior appropriately. This continuous reinforcement should probably continue until the parent's style is between "selling" and "participating" and the maturity of the child shifts toward higher levels (M3 and M4). At that time, the parent should begin to periodically reinforce the child, so that the parent's decreased support and direction will not be seen by the child as punishment. When the style of the parent moves toward a "delegating"style, the child's behavior is self-reinforcing, and external "strokes" from the parent are no longer necessary. In sum, the developmental cycle moves from continuous reinforcement to periodic reinforcement to self-reinforcement.

Be Consistent in Reinforcing Children

In Chapter 2 we defined consistency as behaving the same way in similar circumstances. This is very important when it comes to reinforcement. Many parents are reinforcing or supportive of their children only when they feel like it. While that's probably more convenient for us as parents, it is not helpful if we want to have an impact on our children's behavior. Parents should know when they are being supportive and should be careful not to be supportive when their kids are misbehaving. Be consistent! Only good behavior or improvement, not just "any old behavior," should be rewarded.

Be Careful Not to Reinforce Unwanted Behavior

Problems can result when parents pay attention to their kids only when they are behaving poorly. One couple had all kinds of trouble with a daughter, Cathy, and a son, Peter. They were beside themselves about what they should do. Although they continued to punish both of the kids regularly, Peter and Cathy still misbehaved. When asked what they did when the kids came home from school and behaved well, they responded,

"Nothing! We expect children to be well behaved." In essence, they were saying that they did not pay any attention to "good" behavior.

When people were at their house for dinner or an evening of bridge, it was not unusual for a scene like the following to occur. When Peter would attempt to get the attention of his father (even when he was behaving maturely), his father would say, "Peter, the adults are talking. Don't interrupt." After several futile attempts to get attention from his parents, Peter would go over and punch Cathy in the head. All of a sudden he would have the attention of both his parents. Peter soon learned that if he behaved well, his parents paid little or no attention to him. On the other hand, if he wanted attention from his parents (it was rewarding to him), all he had to do was misbehave. In fact, he became willing to endure what his parents thought was punishment (a spanking) for that attention. So, in the long run, Peter's parents were reinforcing the very behavior they did not want and extinguishing more appropriate behavior.

Positively reinforcing inappropriate behavior is one of the biggest problems parents face; it seems to happen all the time. Have you ever given a crying child a piece of candy? ("Don't cry, dear. Here's some candy.") It works. The child eats the candy and stops crying. But does it really work? The next time the child wants a piece of candy (or our attention) she or he knows exactly how to get it — by crying. We have made the mistake of positively reinforcing inappropriate behavior,[4] which generally results in more of the same.

When's the Last Time We Hugged Our Children?

When our children are growing up, we should be able to say that we have hugged them at least once a day. When we say "hugged" we do not necessarily mean physically. It could very well mean psychologically. Have we given out any "positive strokes" or reinforcement today? There are always going to be parts of our children's lives that need or deserve strokes. If we are not providing some positive strokes for them every day, we probably are not looking hard enough.

The sad thing is that many parents stroke their children the most just after they have punished them. This is particularly typical of the "leave alone — zap" approach to child rearing. Parents using this style leave their children alone until they do something wrong, and then they come down hard on them. When the children start crying these parents feel guilty; after all, "they are so little and we are so big." And the next thing you know, they take a child they have just punished into their arms and comfort the child. Shortly after this scene, they may even do something special with the child like go to the movies. As we suggested in the last section, the child soon learns that the "reward" is worth a little bit of physical pain from a spanking or psychological pain from a "bawling out." What has been reinforced is the crying.

Stroking our children is necessary and helpful, but we need to make sure we do it when they are behaving well, not when we have just punished them.

Isn't All This Reinforcement a Form of Bribery?

The ultimate goal of the developmental process we have been discussing is to shift our children toward self-management, so they can eventually assume responsibility for motivating their own behavior. We mention this "ultimate goal" to reassure those of you who have some real doubts about the use of reinforcement. You may be saying to yourselves, "Children should be motivated by a desire to succeed or the desire to please their parents, not by a hoped-for reward," or "This sounds like bribery to me." Or you may be thinking, "If I use positive reinforcement with my children, won't they grow up expecting rewards for every little thing they do?"

Although we have shared similar concerns in the past, our experiences in observing child rearing have been reassuring. We have found that children who are reinforced early for mature behavior and then gradually are allowed to be more and more on their own turn out to be happy, eager to help, self-motivated kids who can be left alone without "all hell breaking loose." In other words, it seems to work.

In this chapter we have discussed "growing winners" through

a developmental process that emphasizes the use of positive reinforcement. In the next chapter, "What's Good for the Goose May Not Be Good for the Gander," we attempt to help us, as parents, determine what motivates and reinforces each of our children.

4 • What's Good for the Goose May Not Be Good for the Gander

Billy had been thinking about chocolate chip cookies all the way home from school. With every step, he felt hungrier and hungrier. But when he reached home, his mother said, "Billy, I know how hungry you are, but you forgot to make your bed this morning. As soon as it's made, you may have as many chocolate chip cookies as you like. But the bed comes first."

We suggested in Chapter 3 that the key to developing the maturity of our children is understanding what is motivating or reinforcing to each of them. Why?

First of all, the behavior of children is basically goal oriented. In other words, their behavior is generally motivated by a desire to attain some goal or reinforcement.

Second, if children's progress toward directing their own behavior is followed by positive reinforcement ("strokes" — something they desire or need), it is likely they will continue to mature.

Third, what is reinforcing to one child may not be motivating to another. Motivation depends on the strength of a child's needs. Needs are internal wants, drives, or impulses that prompt a person to action. Needs are directed toward goals or hoped-for rewards outside the individual. The interaction between the two evokes behavior,[1] as suggested in Figure 1.

In Billy's case, the goal that could satisfy Billy's need was food. If Billy is dependent on his mother for getting food, his desire for food can be helpful to his mother in influencing Billy's behavior. That is, she can use food to reinforce helpful or mature behavior. In this case, the satisfaction of Bill's need follows making his bed — then he gets his cookies.

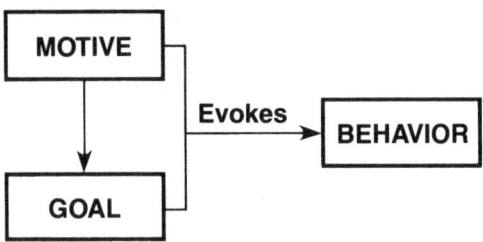

Figure 1. Motives directed toward goals evoke behavior.

With a broad, tangible goal such as food, the type of food that satisfies the hunger motive is likely to vary from situation to situation. If children are really hungry, they may eat anything. At other times, they will be more selective in their goals and only an ice cream cone will do. It should also be remembered that eating is not necessarily a reward — it depends on the strength of the need. Eating for a child like Billy, when he is hungry, certainly is rewarding. But being made to eat when a child is full may be punishing.

Intangible goals like praise can also be reinforcing. If children have a need for recognition — a need to be viewed as "good" kids — praise from parents is one goal that will help satisfy this need. Around the house, if their need for recognition is strong enough, being praised by their parents may be an effective way of getting them to continue to do their chores.

In analyzing these two examples, remember that if we want to influence our child's behavior, we must first understand what needs are most important to our child at that time, as well as what goal can satisfy that need. A goal, to be effective, must be something that the child wants. Thus, parents who are successful in motivating their children to behave in mature, responsible ways generally are good at providing the right goals at the right time.

Striving to satisfy a need leads to behavior. All children have many needs. All of these needs compete for their behavior. What, then, determines which of these needs a child will attempt to satisfy through behavior? The answer is that *the need with the greatest strength* at a particular moment in time leads to behavior. Satisfied needs decrease the need strength, so that less and less behavior is evoked from the need.

The Needs of Children

If the behavior of children at a particular moment is usually determined by their strongest need, it would be very helpful for us to know what needs are commonly most important to children.

Maslow's Hierarchy of Needs

An interesting framework that helps explain the strength of certain needs was developed by Abraham Maslow.[2] He suggested that human needs arrange themselves naturally into a hierarchy, as illustrated in Figure 2.

Physiological needs are highest in the hierarchy, because, until they are somewhat satisfied, they tend to have the highest strength. Physiological needs are basic life-sustaining needs — food, water, shelter. (When we talk about a child's physiological

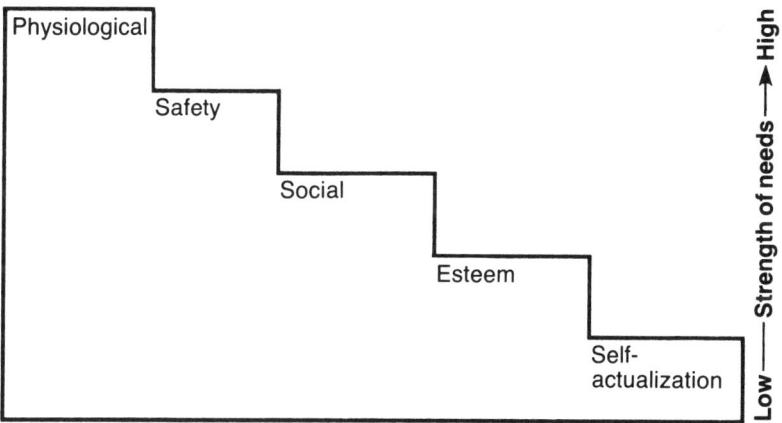

Figure 2. Maslow's hierarchy of needs.

needs not being satisfied, we are not talking about their having a "Big Mac" attack but about real hunger. Deprivation of food at the physiological level means that if a person does not get some nourishment, the body will not function as well as usual. A child can be hungry for a long time before this would occur.) But until the basic needs are satisfied to a sufficient degree, the majority of a child's activity will probably be at this level, and the other levels will provide little motivation. Babies, for example, spend much of their time seeking satisfaction of these basic needs.

But what happens to a child's motivation when these basic needs begin to be fulfilled? As you might expect, other levels of needs become important, and these motivate and dominate the behavior of the child. Then, when these needs are somewhat satisfied, other needs emerge, and so on down the hierarchy.

Once physiological needs are gratified, *safety*, or *security*, needs dominate. These are essentially the need to be free from fear of being killed or hurt physically as well as psychologically. In other words, they are a need for self-preservation. If a child's safety or security is in danger, other things seem unimportant. Nothing can distract the child who fears dogs from holding on to his mother or father and crying "bloody murder" when a dog is around.

Once physiological and safety needs are fairly well satisfied, *social* or *affiliation* needs and the need to be loved will emerge as dominant in the need structure. Since children are social beings, they have a need to belong to and be loved and accepted by various groups, especially their family and friends. When social needs become dominant, children strive for meaningful relations with their parents and friends.

After children begin to satisfy their need to belong to a group and to be loved, they generally want to be more than just a member of their family. They then feel the need for *esteem* — both self-esteem and recognition from others. They want to be involved in the decision-making process in their family and other groups. Most people have a need to be respected by those around them and to be evaluated positively by those they interact with. Satisfaction of these esteem needs produces feelings of self-confidence, prestige, power, and control. When their esteem needs are being fulfilled, children begin to feel that they are useful and have some effect on their environment. There are occasions, though, when children are unable to satisfy their need for esteem through constructive behavior. When this need is dominant, a child may resort to disruptive or immature behavior to satisfy the desire for attention — a temper tantrum is a common ploy. Thus, recognition is not always obtained through mature or adaptive behavior. In fact, many discipline problems may be rooted in children's frustrated esteem needs.

Once esteem needs begin to be adequately satisfied, *self-actualization* needs become more important — that is, the need to maximize one's potential in various aspects of whatever that potential may be. As Maslow expressed it, "What a person *can* be, he *must* be." Thus, self-actualization is the desire to become what one is capable of becoming. Children satisfy this need in different ways. In one child it may be expressed in the desire to be an excellent student; in another it may be expressed by being the "fix-it" person around the house; in another it may be expressed athletically; in still another, by playing the piano.

When self-actualization needs are dominant, Maslow's hierarchy can be illustrated as steps going upward, as shown in Figure 3, rather than downward as in Figure 2. This is because

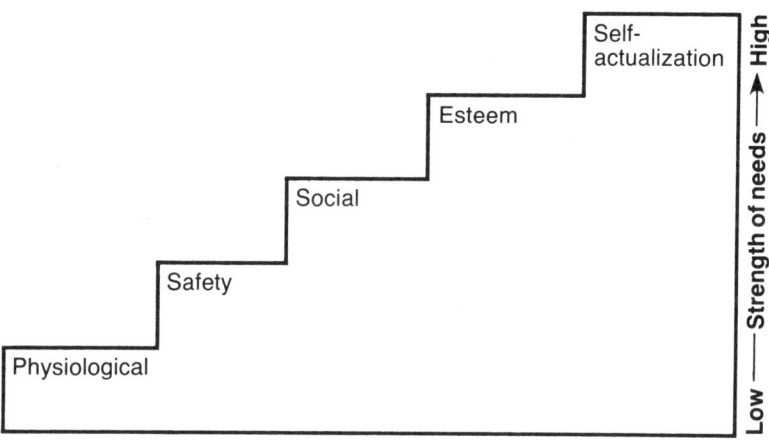

Figure 3. Maslow's hierarchy of needs when self-actualization needs are dominant.

the strengths of all the other needs are now less than the need to self-actualize. Figure 3 is like a frequency distribution. All the needs are evoking a certain amount of behavior, but self-actualization seems to be evoking the most behavior at this moment in time.

We can tell if our child is self-actualizing in a particular area of his or her life if, in that area, the child seems to be confused about the difference between work and play. Inherently, there is no difference between work and play. They both take physical and mental energy. But kids early in life start to label "work" as something that someone else (like a parent or teacher) wants them to do and "play" as something they select to do. Ask almost any elementary-school student (except kindergarteners) what the "best" part of school is and they will usually say "recess." When we ask, "Why recess?", they reply, "Because we can do what we want to do."

Even though this distinction between work and play is clear in the minds of most children, it becomes confused when they are doing something they really enjoy, something that gives them a feeling of self-satisfaction. That can occur even in a traditional work area. The child who is really "into" doing math, like Matt in our example in Chapter 2, will regard his activities in this area as fun. Thus, we should remember that children do not need to self-actualize in all aspects of their lives. In fact, self-actualization in one area often is done at the expense of another area. For example, Glenna might really be maximizing with her piano but not doing very well at school. Another child, Garth, might have no interest in the piano, but be at his best as a student. Our friend Matt seems to be doing the same thing with math and reading.

Self-actualization is not a static concept; the way it is expressed can change as a child gradually matures. For example, a young boy might be self-actualizing when playing and working with blocks, but, eventually, as the child matures, he may look for other areas in which to maximize potential, like athletics or school work. As a child's physical and mental attributes change over time and his or her horizons broaden, new areas of self-actualization emerge.

In discussing the need hierarchy, we have been careful always to say, "If one level of needs has been *somewhat* gratified, then other needs emerge as dominant." The "somewhat" was inserted because we did not want to give the impression that one level of needs has to be completely satisfied before the next level emerges as the most important. In reality, most children as they mature tend to be partially satisfied at each level and partially unsatisfied, with greater satisfaction usually occurring at the physiological and safety levels than at the social, esteem, and self-actualization levels. Therefore, Maslow's hierarchy of needs is not intended to be an all-or-none framework; rather, it is useful in predicting behavior on a high or a low probability basis.

Goals or Reinforcers for Children

Although the hierarchy of needs is helpful in describing the various *internal* needs of children, it does not indicate what *external* goals or reinforcers parents can use to help satisfy each of these needs.

Herzberg's Motivation-Maintenance Theory

The work of Frederick Herzberg and his motivation-maintenance theory[3] come into play when we try to identify goals or reinforcers. In his research on motivation, Herzberg asked people, in all kinds of settings, to describe times on their jobs when they were happy or satisfied and times when they were unhappy or dissatisfied. He found that when people were describing unhappy times, they tended to mention different types of things than when they were talking about happy times. Unhappy times were usually described in terms of things that were happening in their environment, or what Herzberg called *maintenance factors* (these are called maintenance factors because they are never completely satisfied — they have to continue to be maintained). On the other hand, when people were describing times when they were happy, they instead talked about what they were doing (the physical and mental activities they were engaged in), or what Herzberg called *motivators*.

When we ask children these same questions about happy and unhappy times, we get similar results. In describing unhappy times at home, children usually bring up such maintenance factors as the type of *house* they live in; the kinds of *meals* they eat at home; the kind of *bedroom* they have at home; family *rules* or *regulations;* the amount of their *allowance* or *money* available to them; fights with *brothers* or *sisters; how* they are *treated by* their *parents;* their *parents' marital situation* — single, separated, divorced, living together but fighting, etc.; their *position in the family,* i.e., oldest, youngest, etc.

If children are not unhappy with all these environmental aspects of their lives, it does not guarantee they will be mature and responsible, it only means they won't be wasting a lot of time moaning and groaning and complaining.

To grow and develop into mature and responsible individuals, children need to be given opportunities to do things that let them shoulder some responsibility, as well as interesting and challenging activities that, if done well, can bring them recognition (motivation). In describing happy times with their family, children usually talk about such motivators as: *times* when they and their parents were pleased with their *report card; family trips; family building* or fix-up *projects; sports activities with* members of the *family; responsibilities* around the house they *enjoy;* extracurricular *activities* and *honors* at school that *pleased* their *parents* and *themselves; freedoms* and *responsibilities* they were *given by* their *parents,* e.g., baby-sitting themselves, taking the family car on a trip.

The things that make children happy also provide them with opportunities for recognition, for increased responsibility and leadership, and for challenge, achievement, and growth.

The Relationship of Herzberg to Maslow

The work of Maslow and Herzberg can be helpful to us as parents if we recognize that Herzberg's framework describes goals or reinforcers that tend to satisfy the various need levels Maslow described. In particular, environmental (maintenance) factors generally satisfy physiological, safety-security, and social-esteem needs, while the things children do (motivators) tend to satisfy esteem-recognition and self-actualization needs, as shown in Figure 4.

NEED LEVEL	GOALS OR REINFORCERS	
	Maintenance Factors	Motivators
Physiological	Kinds of meals available Amount of allowance or money available	
Safety	Living conditions at home Stability of family—marital status of parents Family rules and regulations	
Social	Relations with brothers and sisters How treated by parents	
Esteem		Activities that can lead to recognition for achievement, such as schoolwork and opportunities for increased responsibility.
Self Actualization		Interesting and self-satisfying activities, such as family outings, creative projects, freedom and responsibility to supervise own activities

Figure 4. Which goals (Herzberg) tend to satisfy which needs (Maslow).

The Herzberg and Maslow frameworks can be used to crosscheck each other, as Figure 4 suggests. Therefore, if we want to influence our children's behavior and we know what their high-strength needs are at a particular time, then by using Figure 4 we should be able to determine what kinds of goals or reinforcers would motivate them. At that same time, if we know our children's goals, we can use Figure 4 to predict what their high-strength needs are.

Maslow's and Herzberg's work share further similarities. Herzberg found that if environmental factors, like Maslow's lower-level needs, are not fairly well satisfied, children, like adults, will care very little about assuming additional responsibilities, even if these responsibilities could bring them higher need satisfaction. For example, children who have unhappy and unpleasant family lives often are not interested in accepting challenges or responsibilities that could help them grow and develop. In fact, they may not even perform up to their present level of maturity and responsibility. Thus, maintenance factors affect the willingness or motivation aspect of maturity, while motivators influence the ability component. In other words, we as parents have to be careful not to have a home environment where our children are very unhappy, because that environment will affect the extent to which they use their present ability. At the same time, we need to provide our children with opportunities for challenge and growth because those *motivators* will affect the extent to which our children will increase their present ability. Let's look at an example.

Susan is highly motivated and is assuming responsibilities around the house appropriate for her age, at say 90 percent of her ability. She is very good baby-sitting for the younger kids in the family, is extremely helpful with household chores, and is respected by everyone. She gets along well with her mom and dad, sister, and two brothers, and is well satisfied with her home and friends. Now, suppose her dad is suddenly transferred and she has to move out of her neighborhood and into a house that is not as nice as the one her family had lived in before. In fact, she has to now share a room with her sister. At the same time, her mom and dad begin to fight a lot, even in front of the kids. How will these factors affect Susan's responsibility around the house?

Since we know performance depends on both ability and motivation, these unsatisfied environmental needs (maintenance factors) may lead to less effort and responsibility. This decline in motivation may be conscious, or Susan may not even realize the change in her behavior. In either case, her responsibility at home may decrease. Even if her family moves back to her old home and neighborhood and her parents start getting along again, Susan's performance or responsibility will probably increase only to its original level.

Conversely, let's assume that the disruptive environment in Susan's life has not occurred at home; she is assuming responsibility at 90 percent ability. Suppose she is continually given an opportunity to develop her ability and satisfy her motivational needs in a home environment where she is increasingly trusted not only to assume responsibility around the house but to make her own decisions, handle her own personal problems without meddling from her parents, and take responsibility for her own behavior. What effect will this situation have on Susan? If she is able successfully to fulfill her parents' expectations and is continually given more and more responsibility and is positively reinforced for her performance on those responsibilities, she may still assume responsibility at home at 90 percent of her ability. But her *total* ability is now increased. As a person, she has matured and grown in self-confidence, and her ability to take on responsibility is also greater than it was.

How Do We Determine the Appropriate Goals or Reinforcers for Our Children?

Although we may now have some idea of what needs are important to our children and what we can use to satisfy those needs, there will be times as a parent when we have trouble identifying reinforcers. We may also find that the reinforcer we have selected is not working. At these times, two tactics can help us select effective reinforcers. One is to be very direct and ask our children what they would like. Their answers are likely to be honest and therefore good indications of what is reinforcing to them. The second way to identify effective reinforcers is to observe what activities our child engages in when given the opportunity to choose. For example, if a mother is trying to identify a reinforcer for her son Doug, she has only to observe what activities Doug chooses to do when he is free to select an entertaining pastime. He may choose to play tennis or ride his bike. These activities are reinforcers for Doug. If Doug's mother wants to increase the amount of homework Doug does, she could promise that if Doug satisfactorily completes an hour or two of homework in the afternoon, he can spend the rest of his time at the tennis court. This will improve his homework behavior.

What Kinds of Reinforcers Can Parents Use?

There are many different types of reinforcers. When children are born, a few things are already reinforcing to them — food and warmth, for example. Babies do not have to learn that these are desirable; they are desirable, in Maslow's terms, for physiological and safety-security reasons. Such automatic reinforcers are called *natural reinforcers*, because they do not have to be learned.

Most reinforcers are not natural: they are learned. Money, music, mother's voice, flowers, trees, vacation, and friends are all learned reinforcers. They are reinforcing because, in the past, children have learned these objects or events are desirable. In child rearing, parents use learned reinforcers most of the time. They may occasionally use food, particularly with young babies, but they will usually rely on people, activities, or things as children get older. In terms of Herzberg and Maslow, things and people tend to be environmental (maintenance factors) and satisfy physiological, security, and social needs, while activities (both physical and mental) involve what children do (motivators) and satisfy recognition and self actualization needs.

Lawrence R. Miller,[4] whose work has been very helpful to us, has compiled a list of reinforcers for children and teenagers. The list may be useful to us as well in attempting to develop the skills and maturity of our children.

Reinforcers for Children

Activities
Television
Movies
Sports events
Parties
Sleep-overs
Camping trips
Fairs
Picnics

Circuses
Going to friend's house
Having a friend over
Staying up late
Choosing TV shows
Horseback riding lessons
Musical instrument lessons
Trip to museum, zoo

Things
New toys
Food
Candy
Bicycle
Sports equipment
Money
Records
Comic books

New clothes
Pets, fish, birds, cats, dogs
Musical instrument
Jewelry
A watch
Books, magazines
Rent for room, furniture
Family taxi service

People Privileges
Time with Mommy, Daddy
Time with friends
Hour, ½ hour, ¼ hour of family member's time
Trips to Dad's or Mom's work

Chores done by brother or sister
Trips shopping with Mom or Dad
Trips with adults on recreation activities

Reinforcers for Teenages

Activities
Television
Movies
Dates
Nights out of house
Use of car
Sports events

Sleep-overs
Dances
Extended hours
Making dinner
Choice of dinner or desserts
Trip to hairdresser, beauty parlor

Trips of choosing
Time at friend's house
Time on telephone

Things
Clothes
Money
Gas for car
Records
Tapes
Phonograph
Radio
Portable radio
Jewelry
Special meals

After school activities
Going out to dinner
Music lessons, riding lessons

Books
Magazines
Pens
Study aids such as a new lamp, chair
Rent on room, furniture, electricity bill
Camera, film
Cosmetics
Money placed in savings account
Musical instruments

People Privileges
Time with friends
Time with girlfriend or
  boyfriend
Having someone else do chores

Hour, ½ hour, ¼ hour of father's,
  brother's, or sister's time

Remember: The purpose of using positive reinforcement is to encourage the development of maturity and independence in our children; positive reinforcement should *never* be used to manipulate and control children for our own ends. Ultimately, we hope to help move our children from a need for external control to self-direction and self-motivation.

Needs/Goals and Parent Leadership Style

If we as parents understand the needs of our children and what goals or reinforcers tend to satisfy those needs, then we can also get a "handle" on what might be the most effective leadership style to use. In fact, Maslow's hierarchy of needs and Herzberg's motivation-maintenance theory can be integrated into our Situational Leadership model. Each of the need levels and the types of goals that will satisfy these needs (maintenance factors or motivators) can be related to the various maturity levels and leadership styles, as illustrated in Figure 5.

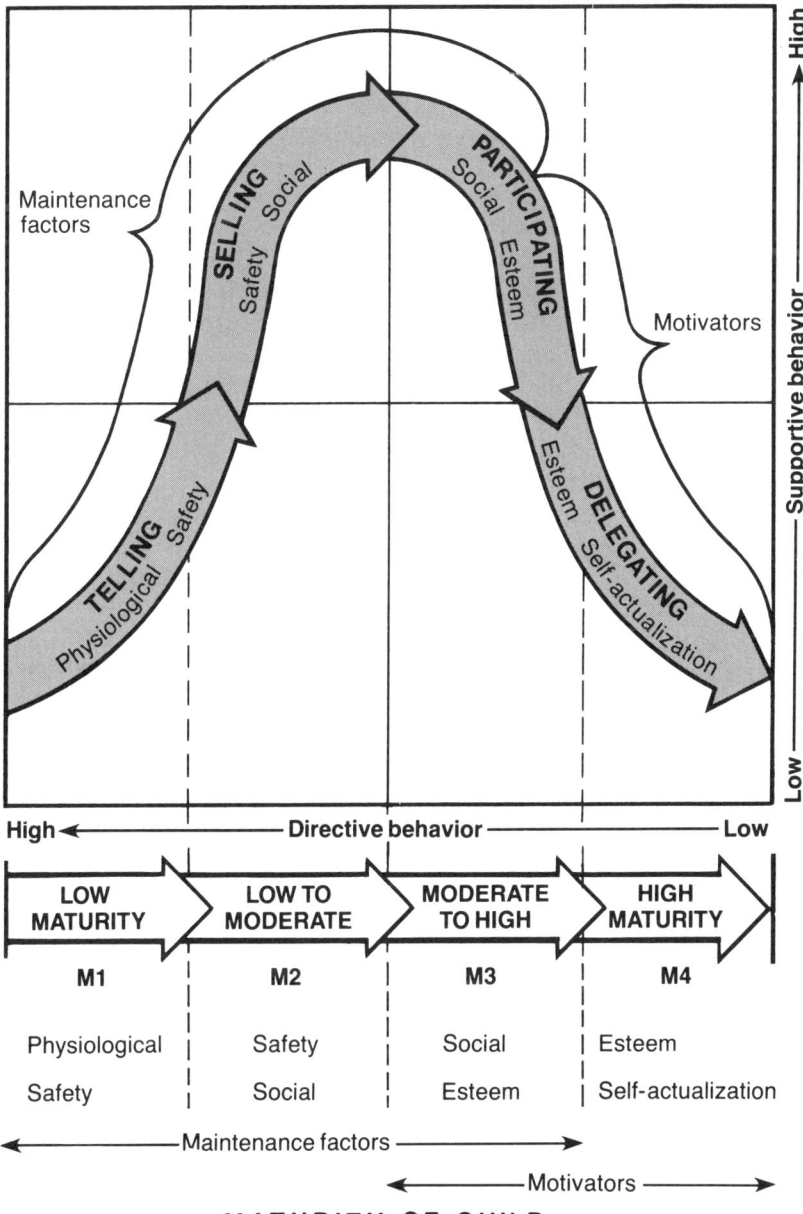

Figure 5. Relationships between Situational Leadership, Maslow's hierarchy of needs, and Herzberg's motivation/maintenance theory.

We can use Figure 5 to plot the styles that are most appropriate for dealing with children motivated by the various high-strength needs described by Maslow and, in doing so, cross-check our analysis of maturity level. As shown in the figure, when children are concerned mainly about physiological needs (often when they are young), their maturity level is usually low (M1); thus, parents can appropriately engage in "telling" behavior (S1), since their child's biggest interest is in getting food. While love and caring are vital always, supportive behavior characterized by two-way communication and positive reinforcement may not be as important at this time. The child needs direction and close supervision *right now* to satisfy his or her basic needs.

When children are no longer concerned about their physiological needs, but instead are motivated by safety-security needs, parents should move to a "selling" style (S2). At this stage, children are still looking to their parents for direction and protection from danger or threats to their security, but they also need supportive behavior to help them overcome these insecurities.

When social-affiliation needs are most important to children, "selling" and "participating" (S3) styles are generally appropriate to use, since children want to belong, be loved, and participate with their parents in family decision making. No longer are they preoccupied with being fed or being safe and secure. Now they want to feel a part of their family.

As esteem and recognition needs move to the fore, children no longer need direction; what they now need is recognition, encouragement, and support from their parents as well as opportunities to take responsibility. Thus, "participating" (S3) is the best leadership mode. Children seeking esteem will work hard and accomplish what needs to be done to get recognition from their parents and others, as well as for their own self-esteem.

Finally, when children are self-actualizing in some aspect of their lives, their parents can adopt a "delegating" (S4) style in that area. Now the children are "doing their own thing" and need little direction or support to sustain their interest or maintain their behavior. They have become self-directed rather than directed by others because their parents have been willing to gradually let them do things on their own.

From this brief overview, you might have gotten the impression that children's needs move from physiological needs to self-actualization with age. While teenage children are, obviously, more often motivated by the higher-level needs than are young children under three or four years of age, need level is not *overall* a function of chronological age. Rather, it is determined by psychological age and by the willingness and ability of children to direct their own behavior in various aspects of their lives.

Again looking at Figure 5, we can also begin to plot the parent styles that are most appropriate for influencing children motivated by maintenance factors (things and people) or by motivators (people and activities). The "telling," "selling," and "participating" leadership styles tend to provide goals consistent with providing a satisfying environment (maintenance factors), whereas the "participating" and "delegating" styles encourage the occurrence of the motivators. What does this mean for us? It suggests that, as parents, we must gradually turn over to our children the direction of their activities, so that they may experience the excitement of inner-directed personal achievement. Their sense of self-worth ultimately should not depend on how they are treated or where they live.

Need Levels and Goals Can Change

When talking about motives or needs and the goals or incentives that can satisfy them, we should keep in mind that a child's need level is not static — that is, just because Joan is being motivated now by a need for esteem, we can't assume that she'll remain at that need level forever.

In fact, circumstances can change quickly, and perhaps next week Joan will be motivated by a need for safety. What exactly happens when the strength of a need changes? Usually, if it decreases in strength, this means it is either satisfied or blocked from satisfaction.

Need Satisfaction

When a need is satisfied by a goal,[5] it no longer strongly motivates behavior and the way is cleared for a competing need to take over. If a high-strength need for Brian, a teenager, is affiliation, being a member of a high school fraternity may lower the strength of this need. Other needs may now become more important to him, like being recognized as a leader. As a result, Brian is likely to strive to become president of his fraternity.

Blocking Need Satisfaction

The satisfaction of a need may be blocked. While a reduction in need strength sometimes follows, it does not always occur initially. Instead, a child may engage for a time in *coping behavior*. This is an attempt to overcome the obstacle by trial-and-error. Thus, if a young girl, Maria, wants to go to a movie with a boyfriend, but her parents say "No," Maria may not give up with this first failure. Instead, she may approach her parents several times with different reasons why she should be allowed to go.

Generally, the more a child strives to reach a goal, the more important that goal becomes. In fact, the strength of the need tends to increase as the child strives for its satisfaction, until the goal is reached (Maria gets to go to the movies) or frustration sets in. Frustration develops when a child is continually blocked from reaching a goal. If frustration becomes intense enough, at least two things can occur: (1) the strength of the need for that goal may decrease until it is no longer strong enough to affect behavior — Maria decides going to the movies is not such a big deal after all; or (2) the strength of the need for that goal may intensify to the point that the child begins to react aggressively by misbehaving or trying to hurt in some way whatever or whoever is blocking the way — Maria becomes angry and calls her parents names. Frequently, when confronted with this irrational behavior, parents make the mistake of giving their children what they want. Thus, when Maria's parents see how upset she is, they relent and let her go to the movies. As we mentioned earlier, this only teaches children how to be disruptive rather than mature in order to get their own way. Maria learns that if she throws a temper tantrum when she does not get her way, her parents will give in.

The strength of a need tends to increase as a child strives for need satisfaction; however, once the child reaches the goal, the strength of the need tends to decrease. In our example, if Maria gets to go to the movies enough with her boyfriend, the need to do that on a Saturday night may decline. When another need becomes stronger than the present need, behavior changes — i.e., Maria wants to go dancing now on Saturday nights.

We've all seen cases similar to the young teenager who wants a car of his own and is willing to work hard during vacations and summers to earn enough money to buy one. The first two weeks he has the car he spends four or five hours a day polishing it until it's the best-looking car in the neighborhood. Gradually, as the weeks go by, he spends less and less time on his car until it looks as dirty as any other car around. What happened? Nothing really — except that he's now into playing the guitar.

Then, of course, there's the "Thanksgiving Day syndrome." As food is being prepared all morning, the need for food increases for children (as well as adults) until the family can't seem to wait to get to the table. As they begin to eat, however, the strength of this need diminishes, especially for the children, who eat as fast as they can. Now, suddenly, after bugging mother all morning for something to eat, they want to be excused from the table only ten minutes after sitting down. Other needs have become more important than food. As they leave the table (if they're permitted), their need for food seems to be well satisfied. They go outside to play ball as the need for active recreation becomes important. But gradually, the need to play outside decreases too. After twenty minutes outside, we find them suddenly in front of the television. Now they want to sit quietly and watch. And eventually, even though their favorite program comes on, the need for passive recreation also declines to the extent that other needs now become more important — perhaps the need to play outside again, or better still, something more to eat. Several hours before they had sworn they could not eat for a week, not even a piece of pumpkin pie, but now that pie looks pretty good. No need is ever completely satisfied; we just satisfy it for a period of time.

Should We Keep Kids Striving — or Satisfy Their Needs?

Is it better to keep children striving for goals or let them reach these goals? Actually, doing one or the other exclusively creates problems. If a child has to work a long time to get anything new (you make him wait a year for a new bike), extreme frustration may cause him to give up working for the goal (he quits helping around the house) or behave in some irrational way, as was true of Maria. On the other hand, if a child always gets his or her own way immediately, the child may lose interest in working for anything. The child's motivation drops, as nothing is challenging anymore. A more appropriate and effective pattern might be a continuous cycle of striving for goals and eventually attaining them.

An appropriate goal for our six-year-old may not be a meaningful goal for the same child when he or she is seven. Once our child becomes proficient in attaining a particular goal, it's up to us to provide an opportunity for evaluating and setting new goals. For example, if our child has learned how to take care of his room, we might now get him involved in helping his older brother take care of the yard.

This cycle of striving for goals and accomplishing goals is a continuous challenge for parents. Parents must keep in tune with their children's progress in the cycle and provide an environment that allows continual realignment of goals. Although at times our role as a parent will be to set goals for our children, this is only part of the story. Equally important is to ensure that our children eventually can play a role in setting their own goals. Research indicates that commitment increases when people are involved in their own goal setting. If children are involved, they will tend to work longer to reach a goal before giving in to frustration. On the other hand, if their parents set the goals for them, they are apt to give up more easily, because they perceive these as their parents' goals, not their own. The movement should be from setting goals for our children to letting our children participate in setting their goals, to permitting our children to set their own goals. Goals should be set high enough so that a child has to stretch to reach them, but low enough so that they can be attained.[6] Thus, goals must be realistic before a child will make a real effort to achieve them. For example, Juanita will not be motivated to work for high grades unless she considers her parents' high expectations realistic and achievable. If she is encouraged to strive for unattainable goals, like being at the very top of her class when it is well known that several kids in the seventh grade have IQ's of 180, then she eventually may give up trying and settle for grades that are lower than she is capable of achieving. In other words, the practice of "dangling the carrot just beyond the donkey's reach," endorsed by many parents for increasing school achievement, may not be a good motivational device.[7]

Another problem with goals is that they often blind us to progress en route — i.e., the person is judged successful only when he or she reaches the end goal. Let's suppose Fred is doing poorly in school and his parents want him to raise his marks to a B average. Suppose that after the first semester Fred gets only C's, and his parents show displeasure and "zap" him. "What's the matter Fred? Thought you were going to get all B's. This is ridiculous. You're sister always got good grades." If this continues to occur there is a high probability that Fred may stop trying. "I can't please the old man anyway, so the hell with it." His grades, instead of improving, may get worse; they go from C's to D's. An alternative for Fred's parents is to set realistic interim goals (remember "Learning a Little Bit at a Time"). Now, any change in the desired direction, even a moderate one, can be positively reinforced. In Fred's case, if some reinforcement is given for his progress (C's), the probability is high that his performance will increase further next semester.

The Effect of Changing Needs on Leadership Style

When a child's need level changes, the leadership style a parent was effectively using may no longer work. Thus, we may correctly be using a supportive "participating" (S3) style in some area where our child only needs to be recognized as competent and capable. Then, suddenly, the situation changes and our child becomes less secure. Now, a shift to "selling" (S2) is needed. Let's look at an example.

The Hendersons were real outdoor types. They especially loved to shoot rapids in a canoe. They spent a lot of time around the water with their children, Sandy and Ken. However, they were reluctant to take them in rapids until they were sure the children could handle a canoe with real skill. Sandy seemed to take to water and to a canoe much more easily than Ken. As a result, when she was twelve they took her with them on their annual shooting of the rapids with old friends. Ken had to stay home; that made him very sad.

The next summer when Ken was eleven he had a chance to go to a YMCA canoe-tripping camp for two weeks. At the camp he went on overnight trips around a series of lakes. The next spring when the family was making plans for their annual trip down the rapids, Ken convinced his folks that he was ready to go. He really felt good about his skills around a canoe after the YMCA experience, and he was anxious to show his mom and dad and be a part of this family outing.

The Hendersons rendezvoused with their friends on Friday night at a selected campsite about three hours from home. That night, after tents were pitched and the group was sitting around the campfire Ken began to hear some rather alarming things, like "Three people have been killed in the rapids over just the last few years."

"What were they doing?" asked Ken. "Couldn't they swim?"

"Sure they could," was the response, "but they were crushed against the rocks by their canoe."

Ken's feelings about the trip suddenly began to change. When he had agreed to come, the needs that were prompting this behavior were esteem needs — recognition from his mom and dad that he could handle a canoe. Now, with the new information, he was slipping from esteem through affiliation to security. Since Sandy had gone on the trip the year before, she tried to reassure Ken that everything was going to be all right.

The next morning was beautiful, warm, and clear. They launched the canoes at a wide part of the river with almost no current. Ken immediately relaxed. The water was just like a lake. "This is going to be a ball," he told Sandy. "I don't know what I was worrying about last night." Ken didn't care where his folks were in their canoe because he felt he and Sandy knew what they were doing and it was a good feeling — the sound of the paddles, the rhythm, the movement.

Then, a muffled roaring ended Ken's calm. He looked around frantically for his folks. "Dad, what's that noise?" he shouted.

"We're approaching our first rapids, Ken." As they came around the bend in the river, Ken couldn't believe his eyes. White, foaming water dotted with dangerous-looking rocks loomed ahead. Ken was petrified. He looked again for his mom and dad and started paddling like the devil to get near them, going at it as if there were no tomorrow.

Soon Sandy and Ken were alongside their parents' canoe and Ken was shouting, "What do we do now, Dad? How are we going to get through this? Shouldn't we turn back?"

His dad, seeing the fear in Ken's eyes, told Sandy and Ken to follow them and not paddle, just steer the canoe. It was a wild ride, but they made it through the first rapids intact.

In terms of Maslow's hierarchy of needs and Herzberg's motivation-maintenance theory, Ken had initially decided to come on this canoe trip to satisfy esteem and recognition needs by joining this family outing and by showing his folks how good he was now in a canoe. But when the situation changed and he found himself in danger, his need level quickly switched to safety and security. No longer was recognition of his skill in a canoe important to him, nor was he interested in being a part of the family outing. At the same time, while he didn't care where his parents were when he and Sandy were paddling on the wide, calm part of the river, he changed his mind very quickly when his safety was threatened. No longer could he tolerate a supportive "participating" style or a leave-alone "delegating" style; he needed both direction and support ("selling"). He needed direction because he didn't know what he was doing, and support to help him start feeling okay again. Luckily, his parents adapted their style to meet Ken's changing need level.

As Ken's case suggests, when a person's need level goes down, his or her performance and maturity (ability and/or willingness to direct one's own behavior) often decreases as well. The problem of what to do when a child's performance begins to decline is a sticky one for parents. In the next chapter, "Stopping Slippage," we show what to do when children begin to misbehave or regress.

Stopping Slippage

A young girl named Nancy was very mature in many areas of her life, especially in helping around the house and doing the chores on her own. As a result, her parents were able to leave her alone ("delegating") in these areas. This mature behavior continued until Nancy reached the "magic" age of thirteen and discovered boys. As a result, her behavior began to change and she started to talk incessantly on the phone and let her chores slip.

In the last two chapters we talked about how to develop the maturity and independence of our children through the use of positive reinforcement and changing leadership styles. In this chapter we discuss what parents need to do when their children begin to regress and behave less maturely than in the past.

The Regressive Cycle

When our children begin to behave less maturely in a particular area than they have in the past, we may need to make a *regressive* intervention. In the regressive cycle,[1] parents use a leadership style appropriate to their child's *present* level of maturity. This differs from the developmental cycle, in which parents attempt to increase the maturity of a child beyond where it has been in the past.

Decreases in maturity are often caused by changing circumstances that rearrange a child's priorities and needs and motivate the child to engage in new, but less responsible, behavior. As we saw in Nancy's case, the impact of adolescence affected her motivation, which changed her behavior and corresponding maturity level in the area of household chores as well as in others (like doing homework) from a high maturity (M4) to a lower maturity level (M3), as shown in Figure 1.

As Figure 1 suggests, if Nancy's parents continued to use a "delegating" style (S4) with Nancy in helping around the house, her performance would continue to decline. Thus, it became necessary for them to shift their behavior initially from style 4 to a "participating" style (S3) to deal with Nancy's decreased maturity. A slight increase in direction and supervision, with significant increases in two-way communication, active listening, and supportive behavior, were called for. This shift to style 3 was appropriate, since Nancy's parents were faced with a motivation problem, not an ability problem. Thus, their first step was to discuss the situation with Nancy and let her participate in coming up with a solution. Then, if Nancy were able to put the problem into perspective and agree on a reasonable solution, her parents could move directly back to a "delegating" style with her in these areas.

Nancy's case helps to clarify one of the basic differences between a developmental cycle and a regressive cycle. In a regressive cycle, once an appropriate intervention has been made, parents often are able to move back to their former leadership style without rewarding small changes in the desired direction, which is characteristic of the process of learning "a little bit at a time." This is because the child already has demonstrated an ability to function at that level.

If, of course, the telephone had continued to disrupt Nancy's behavior in other areas after this "participating" (S3) intervention, her parents may have had to move to "selling" (S2 — high directive and supportive behavior) or even "telling" (S1 — high directive behavior). This would have meant setting down some telephone rules and seeing that Nancy followed them.

The regressive cycle should be taken one step at a time. Thus, if we are letting our child operate on his or her own ("delegating") and performance declines, we should move to "participating" and support the child's problem solving. If we are being supportive but nondirective with our child (S3) and performance

The Regressive Cycle • 103

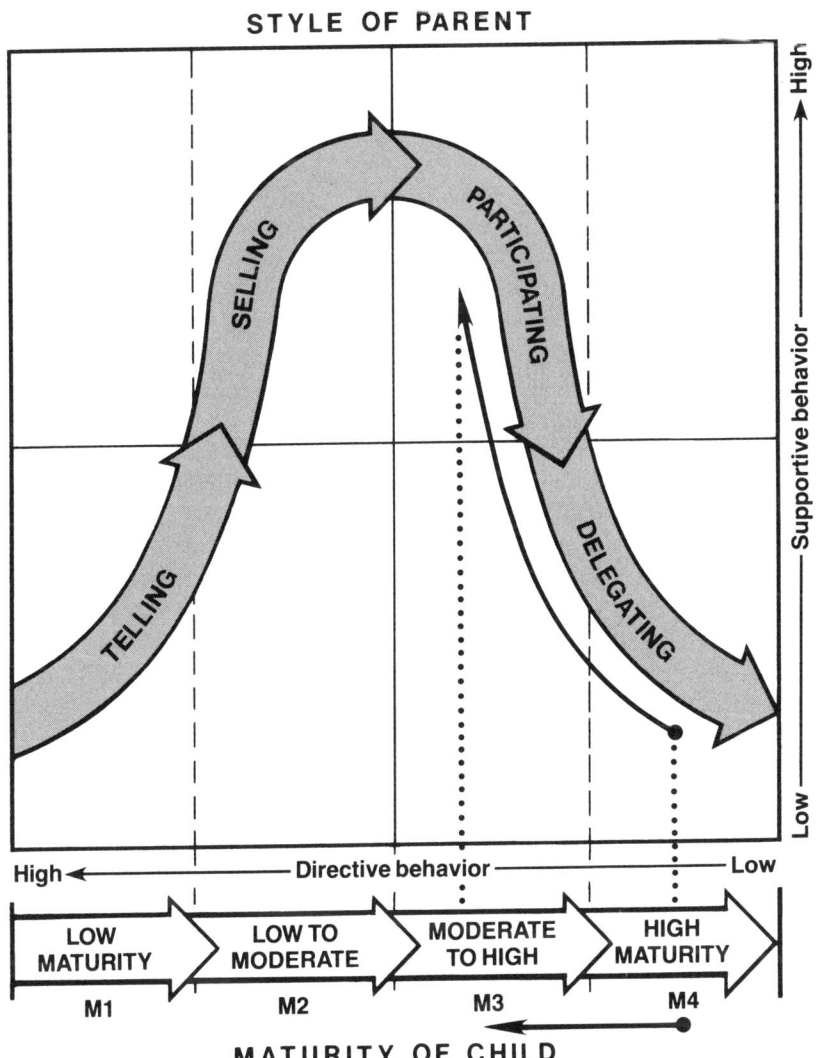

Figure 1. An example of a regressive cycle intervention.

declines, we should move to "selling" and continue to engage in two-way communication, but also be more directive. If we are providing both direction and support (S2) and performance declines, we should move to "telling" and reduce some of our supportive behavior while increasing direction and supervision. In both the regressive and developmental styles, we should be careful not to jump from "delegating" to "selling" or "telling," or from "telling" to "participating" or "delegating." Making a drastic shift backward in leadership style is one of the common mistakes parents make with their children. It sets up the "leave alone − zap (punish), leave alone − zap" style of child rearing, an approach that is not only disruptive to the relationship we have with our child, but is destructive to our child's growth and maturity as well.

The Importance of Timing Interventions

The key to avoiding that disruptive "leave alone − zap" child rearing is the timing of the intervention. The longer we wait to make a move to correct inappropriate behavior and stop a decline in maturity, the further back through the cycle of leadership styles we will have to move and the higher chance that a "telling" (S1) intervention will be necessary. Thus, the earlier you intervene, the better. Both we and our child are likely to be more rational and under control at that point. Nancy's parents, for example, were able to shift effectively from their usual "delegating" style with Nancy back to "participating" because they responded prompty to her telephone problem. Yet this is not the usual case.

Often parents close their eyes to problems and thus delay their interventions. Because they care about their children, or want them to have fun and enjoy themselves, or don't want to rock the boat in their relationship with their kids, they are tempted to excuse their children's inappropriate behavior. Suppose that when Nancy's parents first noticed that Nancy was spending a lot of time on the phone and her chores were not getting done, they decided not to say anything. They were happy that Nancy was so popular and convinced themselves that "this is only a phase; she'll grow out of it, the problem will solve itself."

As a result, weeks and months went by and they still didn't intervene, even though the situation continued to get worse. Now, not only was Nancy letting her chores slip, but she also didn't seem to have time to give her mom a hand with anything. Boys, dates, clothes, and makeup seemed to occupy her mind exclusively. Then, one night months after the problem had begun, her dad's car broke down as he headed home from an evening meeting. After walking a mile to the nearest phone, he tried to call home for his wife to come and get him. Of course, the phone was busy and stayed busy for over an hour straight. Finally, in desperation, Nancy's father attempted to hitchhike, but to no avail. He began the long walk home then, stopping at available phones to call — still busy.

Over three hours from the time he left his office, Nancy's dad entered the house, ripped the phone from the wall, and angrily told Nancy she would never be permitted to make or receive a phone call on a school night again. Since Nancy's parents had never given her a hint that her behavior was "poor," Nancy perceived her father's ravings as unreasonable and totally out of control.

After a shouting match, she ran off crying to her room and slammed the door.

Her father couldn't understand why Nancy was so angry at him, since she was the cause of the problem. And yet, to go from a hands-off "delegating" style to an angrily screaming "telling" style is the ultimate in a "leave alone — zap" child rearing style. Now for the phone problem to be solved, Nancy's parents will probably have to enforce rules that Nancy is not committed to and feels are unfair. While movement to a more directive "telling" style may change her phone behavior, it could kindle feelings of hatred in Nancy for her parents.

This whole confrontation could have been avoided if only Nancy's mom and dad had intervened in the beginning, as we described earlier, when the issue could have been settled in a reasonable manner acceptable to all. We have found that as a general rule "giving birth" is a lot easier than "resurrection." If we would only take the time in the beginning to make sure everything is going "right," we wouldn't have to face the difficult task of "rescue and salvage" when things get off course. A sudden movement from "delegating" (or in this case "abdicating") to "telling" can only lead to a breakdown in parent-child communication and make things "tough" for Nancy's parents.

Avoiding quick style shifts is consistent with a concept that we have undoubtedly heard many times before: "It is easier to loosen up than tighten up." In other words, if we're going to be tough with children in some aspect of their lives, it's better to be tough in the beginning and then, after we see they can handle themselves in that area, loosen up. Children see loosening up as rewarding, but when you tighten up, they are likely to regard it as punishment. An old fable about an emperor and his prime minister illustrates this rather vividly.

When the emperor assumed power he appointed a prime minister. One day he called the prime minister in and said, "Why don't we divide up the tasks? Why don't you pass out all the punishments and I'll pass out all the rewards?" The prime minister, glad to be prime minister, agreed to this. So they did. After a while, the emperor noticed that when he asked someone to do something, the person did it sometimes, but more often didn't. But when the prime minister spoke, people moved. So the emperor called the prime minister to him and said, "Why don't we switch roles for a while? Since you've been doing all the punishing, why don't you do all the rewarding now and I'll do all the punishing?" The prime minister agreed, and they switched roles. Within a month, the prime minister was emperor and the emperor was out on his ear. It seems people didn't take kindly to the "nice guy" turning nasty, and they began to look for a replacement. The logical choice? The prime minister, of course. He seemed to be coming around now and was an alright guy after all.

Is It Ever Appropriate to Move Quickly Backward in Style?

Sometimes, if we do not become aware of a change in maturity until a fair amount of time has gone by, it may be appropriate to move quickly back to a "selling" or "telling" style. For example, suppose our son Paul is normally a good student in school and usually gets B's and A's. Therefore, we have let him handle his school work without supervision. Then, with two weeks left in the grading period, a note from his teacher indicates that Paul has only turned in one problem set in math so far this period. In the grading system the teacher has established, that would not give him a passing grade in math. Good work in five problem sets would be considered a B. In other words, Paul's maturity level in math has moved from a high maturity level (he always got A's in math) to a much lower level (he is now getting an F) during this grading period.

In this situation, if Paul is also concerned about his work in math, it may be appropriate for us to move to a "selling" style (S2) and work closely with him and direct and support his efforts. If, however, Paul seems to "care less" about his poor performance, it would now be appropriate for us to shift our leadership style from "delegating" (S4) to "telling" (S1) to deal with this *drastic* change in Paul's maturity. What might be called a disciplinary intervention would be necessary to redefine expectations and closely supervise Paul during the two weeks he has left to bring his grade up. Since you have expected at least B work from Paul in math and he has always achieved that level, you need to establish some rules and strategies to help Paul complete the required four problem sets in two weeks. Since there is a time pressure, you must move quickly to correct the situation and redirect your son's efforts. This may mean taking away some privileges, like watching TV or playing sports after school. Once this is done and Paul is again able to obtain the desired B level of performance, you might be able to shift your style back to S4. As we noted before, this is possible because Paul has been highly mature in this area earlier. Remember the old story about the mule and the two-by-four? Often, in a disciplinary intervention, all parents have to do to get their children moving back in the right direction is get their attention.

In this situation, if Paul's teacher had given you earlier warning, you may have had some impact at style 3 or 2. Still, we can't blame the teacher entirely. As parents, we must not "abdicate" but rather keep up some two-way communication with our kids (even when we are "delegating") and ask, "How's algebra going?" and so on. Whatever our leadership style, we never go back to zero in terms of supportive behavior and two-way communication. In a "telling" (S1) style we need feedback on how we are doing as the leader of the child, and in a "delegating" (S4) style we need feedback on how the child is doing as his or her own leader.

The Emotional Level of an Intervention

In making an intervention, what level of emotion should a parent use? If we are making a developmental intervention (in other words, attempting leadership with children who have never been any more mature in this area than they are now), we should try to be fairly low key. One common error parents make in using Situational Leadership is assuming that a high-direction "telling" intervention (S1) calls for a raised voice or a threatening tone. This is certainly not the case. Other parents feel that the louder they yell, the faster children will learn.

For example, Gail may quietly tell her son Robbie, "Clean up your room. Your grandparents are coming tonight." Then, an hour later, when Gail discovers Robbie's bed is still messy and his toys are not put away properly, she may resort to yelling (an emotional "telling" style): "I thought I told you to clean your room. Your bed is still a mess and your toys aren't put away!" Now Robbie, realizing that his mother is becoming angry, may leap into action — but unless he knows how to make a bed and where to put his toys, his mother's anger has only made him anxious, insecure, and resentful.

The same situation could have occurred with Paul if he had never really been a good math student. Suppose that when we get word that Paul is doing poor work in math again, we become frustrated. We assume that since he is doing A and B work in all his other subjects, Paul should be getting those kinds of grades in math. Thus, we attempt to deal with his math problem by making a disciplinary intervention (we "zap" him). "What's the matter with you, Paul? You're not doing the kind of job in math that we know you can. It looks to me like you're getting lazy! I don't want any more TV watching until you get this math thing squared away! Understand?"

This disciplinary intervention is quite emotional. Since Paul has never been any more mature in math, this kind of intervention may actually increase the chances of Paul losing interest in math entirely. Math now represents higher levels of anxiety and it is less likely that we will be able to motivate Paul in this area.

What should we have done? An appropriate intervention with Paul would be a developmental cycle, where we increase direction and supervision without displaying anger or disappointment. This might take the form of talking with his teacher to set up a math tutorial in school, along with closer supervision of Paul's progress and additional homework assignments that you could monitor and assist him with. All these activities should be carried out calmly and supportively, so that Paul will not become frightened or excessively anxious. The simple lesson to be learned from all this is to avoid making an emotional disciplinary intervention when our child lacks the ability to do the task in the first place. Such an intervention could have damaging results. We can do a lot of telling what to do, where to do it, and how to do it (S1) without losing control of our emotions.

Is an emotional "telling" intervention ever appropriate? Consider the following two contrasting situations. Bryan, a parent coach of the neighborhood basketball team, has a big, awkward son named Pearson who has trouble catching a basketball, much less putting it in the basket. Obviously, a high emotional reaction to mistakes by this boy would not help him develop, since he does not yet know how to play. If his father pulls Pearson out of a game every time he makes some mistake and begins yelling at him, Pearson is likely to avoid the ball altogether when he gets back on the court. While Pearson needs a lot of direction and supervision, it should be presented in a way that helps to develop his confidence rather than increase his insecurities.

On the other hand, if the father's other son, Greg, a boy with proven athletic ability, begins to "goof off" during a game, his father might want to make a disciplinary intervention. With this kind of intervention it sometimes is appropriate to be more emotional and even display a moderate amount of anger. If earlier less-directive attempts have failed with Greg, this directive style may be needed to make Greg realize that he is not using his ability and motivation enough. Once this happens, Greg can go back in the game and start performing well without any further direction from his dad. Keep in mind, of course, that too much emotion becomes dysfunctional, even in a disciplinary cycle.

Some Things to Remember when Disciplining a Child

If a disciplinary intervention is called for, how can it be carried out effectively? Here are a few helpful guidelines.[2]

Don't blow your cool: As we suggested above, even when making a disciplinary intervention, we should remain relatively calm and use only a moderate level of emotion. Keep the emotional level only high enough to get the child's attention; make it obvious that a problem exists, but don't get "carried away."

Don't attack personalities: When disciplining a child, don't attack the child's worth as a human being. Separate the child as a person from the child's behavior. The child is OK, but his or her behavior is not. Zero in on that behavior and not on the child.

Be specific: It's not very helpful to a child to say, "I don't like the way you have been behaving lately." That kind of feedback is too general. For a disciplinary intervention to be effective, we must tell the child specifically what he or she has done wrong, i.e., "You didn't do the dishes, you fought with your sister, or you talked back to me."

Be timely: We have already emphasized the importance of timing your interventions. Unless discipline occurs as close to the misbehavior as possible, it won't be helpful in influencing future behavior. Some parents are "gunnysack" discipliners. That is, they store up observations of poor behavior and then one day when the "bag is full" they charge in and "dump everything on the table." They tell the child all the bad things he or she has done for the last few weeks or months or more. Parent and child usually end up yelling at each other about the "facts" and the child doesn't really hear what he or she has done wrong. This is a version of the "leave alone — zap" form of discipline. If parents would only intervene early, they could calmly deal with one behavior at a time and the child could "hear" the feedback.

Be consistent: Parents should avoid inconsistency in their disciplining of children. The same behavior should always be met with the same response. A child will become confused if he is scolded for fighting with his sister in the car and ignored when he does the same thing in the supermarket. We must also be careful to treat one son or daughter the same as another son or daughter. Be careful not to have "favorites."

Don't threaten: So many parents announce in ominous tones that they are going to do such and such if a child continues to misbehave, and then never follow through. If our children realize we are bluffing, they won't pay any attention to our threats. Then, when we finally do follow through on a threat, we are usually so out of control that we come down excessively hard. So, quite simply, "say what we mean and mean what we say."

Be fair: Parents should be careful not to make a punishment greater than the problem, and vice versa. Many parents come down harder on their children for little things than for more major "crimes." If children know what is expected of them and they don't do it, they will readily accept punishment (in fact, they sometimes are confused if they don't receive it). But if the punishment is way out of proportion to the misbehavior, they will justifiably resent their parents' response.

Be careful that discipline does not reinforce poor behavior. As we discussed in Chapter 3, sometimes the only way children can get their parents' attention is by misbehaving. If that's true and attention from their parents is important enough to them, they may behave inappropriately just to be recognized, even if they get disciplined and have to "pay a price" in the bargain.

Is It Really OK to Punish Our Children?

When we punish a child, we are following some behavior with a consequence the child would not choose — e.g., a scolding, a spanking, or having a privilege taken away. Some parents have been told that they should not punish their children, that it will damage them psychologically.

As our discussions about level of emotion and discipline in this chapter suggest, we are not against the use of punishment when it's appropriate — like removing Paul's TV privilege when he brings home an F grade in math after being an A student the semester before. Yet we must realize that punishment has at least two limitations.

First, *punishment does not teach children what to do*, it only shows them what *not* to do. Thus, like a high level of emotion, punishment is not a useful technique to use when children don't know what to do in an area. In that area, they need directive coaching and counselling appropriate for the early stages of a developmental cycle. During this stage, we should positively reinforce any progress made in the direction of the desired behavior. If children are continually punished for not doing something that we or someone else (a teacher, etc.) has never taught them, they are likely to become frustrated and angry enough to either strike out at the person doing the punishing, retreat into themselves, or engage in behavior that is not directed toward goal accomplishment but is intended to avoid the punishment.

Second, sometimes *the avoiding of the punishment can reinforce behavior we don't want.* A vivid example of an unwanted behavior being reinforced was related to us by friends who got a new puppy for Christmas. They had a strategy to housebreak the dog. Their plan was that when the puppy had an accident in the house, they would put his nose in it, smack him on the tail with a newspaper, and toss him out the kitchen window onto their back deck (they live in California). We laughed as they told us, because we had a good idea what must have happened (our only concern was how high the dog could jump). As we guessed, within three days the dog would do a "job" on the floor and then jump out the window. The dog didn't know where to do it; all he knew was that if he did it, he better clear the area. The same thing happens when parents use a lot of punishment or guilt in toilet training young children. After a while, the children will hide when they have gone in their pants or deny to a parent that they have done so.

When our friends realized what was happening, they began taking the dog for walks in shifts (everybody in the family had a turn or two). They would follow him everywhere. After he squatted or lifted his leg, the person who was with him showered the puppy with love and dog biscuits. The puppy soon would scratch on the door to go out. Gradually, from reinforcing the dog every time he asked to go out, the dog became completely house trained. A similar use of positive reinforcement is being employed by the parent who waits patiently in the bathroom with a child during toilet training.

Does It Ever Help to Ignore a Decline in Maturity?

If our child begins to behave less maturely than in the past and we ignore this decline, our child's new behavior is said to be "on extinction" (we stay at S4 and don't intervene). Punishment tends only to suppress behavior; extinction tends to make it disappear. To extinguish a response, we must purposely withhold both reward and punishment (nothing must happen as a result of behavior). For example, suppose a young child, Kitty, finds that whenever she stomps up and down and cries, she gets the attention of her parents and usually receives something she wants, like a cookie. Now, if her parents don't want that kind of behavior, they could extinguish it by not responding to Kitty at all. After a while, when Kitty sees that her stomping and crying doesn't get her anything, she'll do it less and less often. People seldom continue to do things that do not provide positive reinforcement.

As we suggested in Chapter 3, some parents have problems with extinction because they tend to pay attention to their kids only when they are behaving poorly. If this attention is important enough to the kids, they soon recognize that "the only way you get any time around here from Mom and Dad is to cause trouble." This could occur with Kitty, the stomper and crier, if she always receives a cookie for disruptive behavior but gets "no action" when she is behaving well. This use of supportive behavior (S3) with inappropriate behavior and "leave-alone" behavior (S4) with good behavior (when that behavior is not self-reinforcing) generally results in more unwanted behavior.

When to Use Punishment or Extinction

In essence, what we are saying is that it's essential to think before we act, because we never know what we may or may not be reinforcing in our children. This is particularly true when it comes to using punishment and extinction. And yet, both of these can be useful in unfreezing inappropriate behavior, so that we can begin to positively reinforce more desirable behavior.

In using punishment or extinction, it's important to know what behavior we want to change and to communicate that in some way to our child. To determine when to use punishment and when to ignore (extinguish by withholding reinforcement), we need to estimate how long the undesirable behavior has been occurring. If the behavior is new, ignoring it (extinction) may get results. But if the behavior has been occurring for some time (and we haven't done anything about it), it may be necessary to suppress the behavior through some form of punishment. Only then can we redirect our child so that the desired behavior can begin to increase through positive reinforcement. Again, the longer we wait, the more difficult it will be to change an unwanted behavior.

In this chapter, we have attempted to help develop some strategies for turning around a decrease in maturity. In the next chapter, "Monkey Business," we discuss how we can identify and solve child-rearing problems in a way that keeps our children growing and developing their own problem-solving skills.

6 • *Monkey Business*

The Fishers were extremely proud of their daughter Sharon. She had really pitched in to help when her mother decided to go back for her master's degree at the local university. Lately, though, Sharon hadn't been coming home in time to help with dinner. And her bed had gone unmade for a week. Sharon's mom and dad weren't quite sure what, if anything, to do.

As we suggested in the last chapter, effective parents are not only able to develop the maturity and independence of their children, they are also able to spot "slippage" in maturity and intervene early enough to turn the situation around. How can we, as parents, know when to intervene? What should we look for?

As a simple guideline, whenever we receive feedback, either verbal (our child tells us) or nonverbal (we observe our child's behavior), indicating that our child is having a problem in some area, it's time to think about stepping in. A *problem* exists when there is a difference between what our child is doing and what we and/or our child think he or she should be doing. Thus, detecting problems is all-important in determining what areas of our child's life require our attention.

Problem Ownership — Who's Got the Monkey?

In his book *Parent Effectiveness Training* (PET),[1] Thomas Gordon argues that one of the most important steps in becoming

more effective in raising responsible, self-motivated children is determining whether their behavior is acceptable or unacceptable to us as well as to them. Once the acceptance question has been answered, then it is important to determine "who owns the problem" — that is, who is most "bugged" by the unacceptable behavior.
Combining this concept of "who owns the problem?" with William Oncken, Jr.'s helpful "monkey-on-the-back" analogy,[2] there are four potential "monkey business" (problem) situations.

1. *The parent has a "monkey"* — the child's behavior is a problem to the parent but not to the child. Thus, the "monkey" is on the parent's back.
2. *Both parent and child have a "monkey"* — the child's behavior is a problem to both the parent and the child. Thus, both have a "monkey."
3. *The child has a "monkey"* — the child's behavior is a problem to the child but not to the parent. Thus, the "monkey" is on the child's back.
4. *Neither parent nor child has a "monkey"* — the child's behavior is a problem to neither parent nor child. There is no problem, the "monkey" is gone.

Situational Leadership and Monkey Business

If we can identify who has the monkey, then we are in a position to determine which leadership style has the best chance of success and thus when and how to intervene with our child in each of the four problem situations. As Figure 1 suggests, acceptable or unacceptable behavior can be associated with our concept of maturity.

If the behavior of a child is acceptable to a parent, it represents moderate to high levels of maturity (M3 and M4), and thus a parent can use a "participating" (S3) or "delegating" (S4) style. However, if the behavior of a child is unacceptable to a parent, it represents low to moderate levels of maturity (M1 and M2), and thus a "telling" (S1) or "selling" (S2) parental style is appropriate.

To further differentiate between "telling" and "selling"

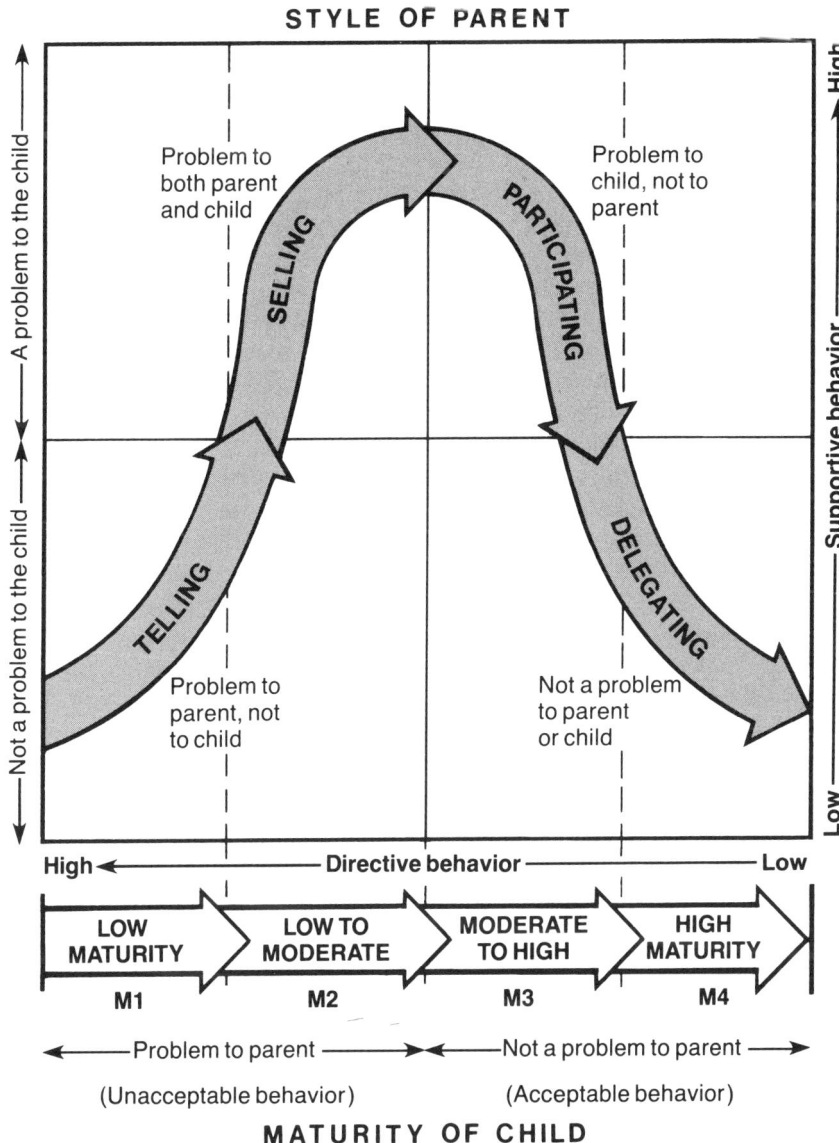

Figure 1. Situational Leadership and its relationship to problem ownership.

or "participating" and "delegating," we need to determine who has the monkey. Imagine that we are confronted with a problem that we don't quite know how to handle. As Figure 1 illustrates, if we look at who has the monkey, we can begin to determine whether we should take action and, if so, what leadership style would be appropriate with each of the four problem situations.

First, if the behavior of our child is acceptable to both ourselves and the child, the most appropriate parental leadership style is "delegating" (S4). Since there is no monkey, no intervention is necessary.

If, however, our child's behavior is acceptable to us but is a problem to our child — maybe because of peer pressures or other pressures that cause the child to question his or her behavior — the appropriate leadership style is "participating" (S3). Since our child has a monkey, we must engage in a lot of supportive behavior, active listening, and two-way communication to maintain the present acceptable behavior. Regrettably, parents often treat this problem situation as if there were no problem. Since they aren't bothered, they see no reason to act. If a supportive intervention is not made here, however, there is a high probability that the situation will become a problem to both parent and child. For example, Martha, a junior in high school, is avoiding the use of drugs. Since she is not using drugs, her behavior is not a problem to her parents. However, her behavior may be a problem to Martha herself, since all her friends are involved with drugs and are pressuring her to join them — that is, "Get with it or forget being a part of our crowd." If her parents treat this situation as if there was no monkey, it may quickly become a problem to both. The competing pressures at school combined with no support or active listening at home could push Martha toward drugs and acceptance by her peers. Thus, by not making a supportive "participating" (S3) intervention at the appropriate time, Martha's parents have helped to create a monkey for all involved.

If our child's behavior is unacceptable and therefore a problem to us but not to our child, it's not necessary for us to provide support. In this situation, since our child sees no problem, we must provide some direction. Since the monkey is on our backs, we merely need to make clear to our child where the limits are (a "telling" [S1] intervention). At this stage, fifteen or twenty minutes spent in discussing how we view the "problem" is a waste. Remember, the child doesn't see any problem. He or she just wants to know what the rules are so that he or she can behave accordingly.

For example, in telling his teenage son Jim when to get home on a Friday night, a father may indicate 11:30, 11:45, or even midnight. That doesn't really matter to Jim; any of those times are okay. All he wants to know is what his dad expects — he doesn't want to sit around and talk about it. If, after his dad indicates what he expects, Jim readily accepts it, then his father can go directly from "telling" (S1) to "delegating" (S4).

If, however, Jim's dad suggests a 10:00 curfew and this seems unreasonable to Jim, the situation might quickly become a problem to both. Now that both Jim and his father have a monkey, his dad can't jump directly to "delegating." He has to move to S2 and engage in "selling" behavior rather than "telling." He has to open up channels of communication and engage in facilitating and "stroking" behaviors, getting Jim to understand the "why" of the early time and psychologically "buy in" to the decision. Jim's father might say, "Your two cousins are coming tomorrow and we have a big day planned at the beach, so I'd like you home early tonight. Next Friday, though, you can stay out until 11:30." In other words, Jim's father attempts to make some trades to smooth the interaction and get Jim to agree to the decision.

Finally, if our child's behavior is unacceptable and both we and our child have a monkey, the appropriate leadership style for us is "selling" (S2), since the child needs some directing. Yet, because our child also sees the behavior as a problem, it's equally important to keep open the lines of communication. Now we are into mutual problem solving with our child.

We think this integration of Situational Leadership with monkey business and problem ownership can be helpful to us in deciding when and how to intervene in our children's affairs. Remember, even if our child's behavior is acceptable to us, we still may have to take action if our child needs support and encouragement to keep up the good work. If our child's behavior is unacceptable to us, a more directive intervention is needed to turn the situation around. How directive the intervention must be ("telling" or just "selling") depends on whether our child also sees this behavior as a problem.

Transactional Analysis

By integrating Situational Leadership with problem ownership and monkey business, we attempted to help parents analyze when and how they should intervene in problem situations so that they can avoid a serious regression in their child's behavior. While using the leadership style with the greatest chance of success may help turn the problem situation around, we can't guarantee it because the response of a child to a parental intervention is not always predictable. That is why we have been careful throughout this book to talk about the style with the *highest probability* of success for a given situation, not necessarily a magic solution.

If it is true that we cannot always anticipate the reaction of a child to a parental intervention, how can we better predict the kinds of responses our interventions may evoke from our children? *Transactional Analysis* (TA), a method of analyzing the communication patterns and transactions that occur between people, may help us in this area. This school of thought was developed by Eric Berne[3] and, in more recent years, has been popularized by the work of such people as Thomas Harris, Muriel James, Dorothy Jongward, and Abe Wagner.[4]

TA, as we view it, is an outgrowth of Freudian psychology. Sigmund Freud[5] was the first to suggest that three sources within the human personality stimulate, monitor, and control behavior. The Freudian id, ego, and superego are important concepts, but their definitions are difficult for parents to understand or apply without extensive training in psychotherapy. Thus, one of the major contributions of TA theorists is to have put some of Freud's concepts into a language that everyone can understand. Without being trained psychiatrists, any of us can use TA terminology to better grasp why people behave as they do.

According to TA, a *transaction* is a stimulus plus a response. For example, if you say to your son, "You really look nice today, Don," that's a stimulus; if he says, "Thanks," that's a response. Thus, transactions take place between people. They can also take place between the "people" in our heads. If we have a sudden impulse to say something to someone, we may mentally hear a voice telling us not to say it and a second voice agreeing. These people in our heads are called *ego states*.

The personality of a person is the collection of behavior patterns developed over time that other people begin to recognize as that person. These behavior patterns are evoked in differing degrees from three ego states — PARENT, ADULT, and CHILD. These terms are capitalized so as not to be confused with their lower-case counterparts. Thus, a parent (mother or father) has PARENT, ADULT, and CHILD ego states; and a child (son or daughter) also has PARENT, ADULT, and CHILD ego states. These ego states have nothing to do with chronological age, only psychological age. As Berne states, "Although we cannot directly observe these ego states, we can observe behavior and from this infer which of the three ego states is operating at that moment."[6] The three ego states are usually diagrammed as in Figure 2.

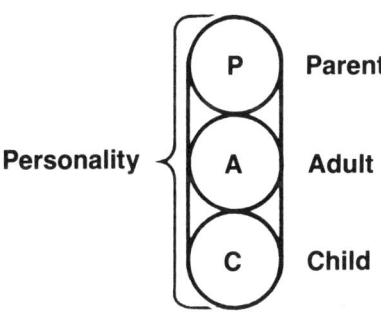

Figure 2. The personality includes Parent, Adult, and Child ego states.

The CHILD Ego State

The CHILD ego state is associated with behaviors that appear when a person is responding emotionally. A person's CHILD contains the "natural" impulses and attitudes learned from child experiences. The two kinds of CHILD ego state we use are *Happy CHILD* and *Destructive CHILD*.

Children behaving from their Happy CHILD are doing things because they want to, but their behavior is not disruptive to others or destructive to the environment. Children in their Destructive CHILD are also doing things because they feel like it, but their behavior is either disruptive to others or destructive to themselves or their environment. In understanding the difference between these two types of CHILD ego state, it helps to remember that behavior by itself is not happy or destructive. Whether a child's behavior is coming from the Happy CHILD or Destructive CHILD depends on the transaction or feedback from others. For example, if George is singing in the shower, he may be in his Happy CHILD. But if his sister Helen tells him she is having trouble studying because of his singing and he keeps on singing, he has moved from Happy CHILD to Destructive CHILD.

Sometimes, one form of the Destructive CHILD ego state is the *Rebellious CHILD*. When children are in this ego state, they aren't going to listen to anyone who tells them what to do. They either rebel openly by being very negative or rebel subtly by forgetting, being confused, or putting off doing things that someone wants them to do.

Another CHILD ego state sometimes mentioned is *Compliant CHILD*. When children are in this ego state, they do what others want. Complying with the wishes of others is okay if the child really wants to do that or if it makes sense to do it. When that is the case, Compliant CHILD would be classified as a form of Happy CHILD because the behavior would not be considered disruptive to others or destructive to themselves or their environment. However, Compliant CHILD can hurt the development of children who comply unquestionably all the time, even when it makes no sense to them. These children tend to remain dependent rather than become independent. When this occurs, Compliant CHILD becomes a form of Destructive CHILD.

It is healthy for people to have a functioning CHILD ego state that is spontaneous, emotional, and sometimes dependent. However, as parents, we want to discourage too much development of our children's compliant or rebellious forms of Destructive CHILD.

When and how do children develop a Rebellious CHILD ego state? Children start learning the behavior associated with this ego state when they are very young from the way they are treated by their parents. Let's look at an example of a baby whose mother and father both work full time. During the day, they have delegated babysitting to a day care center, grandparents, or a babysitter in their home. When they get home, they are often very tired and they'd like to sit down, relax, have a drink, and talk to each other. If the baby is in his crib and being "good" (that is, lying on his back looking at the plastic birds and "cooing"), the father is apt to say to his wife, "Don't go near the baby! Don't go near the baby!" In other words, the baby is being "good" and they want to relax, so they "don't rock the boat." "After all," the father may say, "we'll probably be up two or three times during the night caring for the baby, so let's leave well enough alone for now."

What the father doesn't realize is that the baby soon learns (even though not old enough to communicate in words) that the only way he gets any attention or "strokes" from his mom or dad is to scream, holler, and raise hell. Then his mom or dad will run over, pick him up, cuddle him, and try to find out what is wrong. When parents pay attention to their children only when they are disruptive, as we discussed in Chapter 5, they tend to be positively reinforcing negative behavior, which will increase the frequency of that behavior. If this is done enough, the child will begin to develop his or her destructive, Rebellious CHILD ego state.

If parents want to avoid too much Rebellious CHILD in their youngsters, they must learn to respond positively to good behavior. The time to pick up and cuddle a baby is when that child is playing and behaving well, not when he or she is screaming and yelling for no good reason, such as when you know the baby has just eaten and been changed. It is interesting to note how many parents who positively reinforce disruptive behavior in their children as babies continue to do it as they get older. Take, for example, the father who is watching an "important" NFL football game on TV with some friends when his ten-year-old son comes into the room and starts "causing trouble." How will the father react? Like so many parents, he may take the easy way out and reach into his pocket and give the boy three dollars to go to the movies with a friend. A parent who does this kind of thing avoids dealing with the problem in the short run but in the long run has reinforced the kind of behavior that will result in a well-developed Rebellious CHILD ego state and problems later on.

When and how do children develop a Destructive Compliant CHILD ego state? Children become docile and compliant when their parents never veer from a "telling" (S1) style of leadership. These parents have the philosophy that children should be "seen but not heard" and should do what they are told at all times. As we discussed in Chapter 2, children who are always treated in a "telling" manner will either become openly antagonistic toward their parents and get out from under their control as soon as possible (a Rebellious CHILD) or become passive, docile, and dependent (a Compliant CHILD).

If parents want to avoid making their children too compliant but still want them to comply when it makes sense, they must learn to use the more supportive "selling" and "participating" styles as their children begin to become more mature. In our TV football game example, the father might take his son aside and explain the situation to him and ask him to play somewhere else during the game, agreeing to do something special with him after the game if he is able to entertain himself constructively until then.

The PARENT Ego State

The PARENT ego state is a result of the kind of "messages" people received from their parents, older sisters and brothers, school teachers, Sunday school teachers, and so on during their early childhood. These messages can be thought of as recorded on "little cassette tapes" in people's heads. They're in place, stored up, and ready to go — all you have to do is push the right button and you get the message almost like you do when you dial a certain number on the phone. Push another button and you get a different message. After the message is given, the tape is rewound and ready to go again. For instance, if a father's son wasn't eating his dinner and was playing with his food, a very common PARENT tape like the following might be played: "Stop playing with your food, Garth, and clean up your plate. People are starving all over the world, so you're going to eat everything." Now where did the father learn to say that? He probably learned it from his mother and father, who learned it from their parents. And now he's laying it on his kids. This is a PARENT tape. Many of us were taught when we were young that it's "good" to clean our plate and "bad" to leave food on our plate. In fact, if we are honest with ourselves, many of us probably still feel guilty today if we leave food on our plate.

Thus, a person is operating from a PARENT ego state when he or she mentally plays back "old tapes" from childhood. These "recordings" say such things as "It's right!" "It's wrong!" "It's bad!" "It's good!" "You should!" "You shouldn't!" Thus, our PARENT ego state is the evaluative part of us that evokes value-laden behavior. But remember, this value-laden behavior is not necessarily "real value" — it's "learned value." In our example with Garth not cleaning his plate, it might be more appropriate for his father to say, "Don't feel you have to eat everything on your plate if you're really not hungry" — particularly if he is a little overweight. Thus, cleaning one's plate is a "learned value" because, in a real sense, whether or not Garth eats all the food on his plate won't really impact starving children around the world, it will only impact the size of the garbage.

There are two kinds of PARENT ego states, *Nurturing PARENT* and *Critical PARENT*. The Nurturing PARENT is that part of a person that is understanding and caring about other people. While behavior coming from the Nurturing PARENT may set limits on and provide direction for people's behavior, in so doing it will not put these people "down" and make them feel not OK as individuals.

The Critical PARENT makes people feel that they, not just their behavior, are not OK. Thus, Critical PARENT behavior attacks a person's personality as well as his or her behavior. The Critical PARENT tends to "put down" the Happy CHILD ego state in our head as well as the CHILD in others. When people are in their Critical PARENT ego state, they are very evaluative and judgmental. They are always ready to respond with a "should" or "ought" to almost anything people tell them.

The ADULT Ego State

The ADULT ego state evokes behavior that could be described simply as logical, reasonable, rational, and unemotional. ADULT behavior is characterized by problem-solving analysis and rational decision making. In TA terms, when our ADULT is in the "executive position" of our personality, we are thinking before we act. The ADULT ego state takes the emotional CHILD ego state and the value-laden PARENT ego state and checks them out in the "real" world. When we are in our ADULT, we examine alternatives, probabilities, and values prior to engaging in behavior.

ADULT behavior is quite different from CHILD behavior. CHILD behavior is often behavior that's almost a stimulus-response relationship. Something happens and the person responds almost immediately. What happens is not processed intellectually. It almost goes "in one ear," picks up speed, and goes "out the other ear." With ADULT behavior, when something happens, there is not an immediate response. A response follows only conscious evaluation and thought.

A Healthy Personality

All parents and children behave from these three ego states at different times. A healthy person has a personality that maintains a balance between all three, particularly Nurturing PARENT, ADULT, and Happy CHILD. This means that these people are able, at times, to let the ADULT ego state take over and think very rationally and engage in problem solving. At other times, these people are able to free up the CHILD ego state and let their hair down, have fun, and be spontaneous and emotional. At still other times, healthy people are able to defer to the PARENT ego state and learn from experience — they do not have to "reinvent the wheel" every time. They develop values that aid in the speed and effectiveness of decision making.

While a balance between all three ego states seems to be most healthy, some people (both parents and children) seem dominated at times by one or two ego states. This is especially a problem when the ADULT is not in the "executive position" and a person's personality is being dominated by the Critical PARENT or the Destructive CHILD. When this occurs in children, it poses problems for their parents on a day-to-day basis.

More specifically, CHILD-dominated kids (as well as parents), who are mainly coming from Destructive CHILD, do not engage in much rational problem solving. They learn in their early years that they can get things by screaming, hollering, and being emotional. It's very difficult to reason with them in many situations. Rather than solve their own problems, these children want their parents or some other adult to tell them what to do, where to do it, and how to do it or what's right, what's wrong, what's good, and what's bad.

PARENT-dominated children (as well as parents), who are mainly coming from Critical PARENT, also do not engage in much rational problem solving because they already know "what's right" and "what's wrong." They seem to have an answer for everything. These children we would characterize with the comment, "Look! Don't confuse me with the facts, I've already made up my mind." It really doesn't matter how much real information anyone brings to these children; they've already decided "It's good," "It's bad," "You should," or "You shouldn't."

Even ADULT-dominated children (as well as parents) can be troublesome, because they can be very boring to live with. They don't seem to act like other kids. They are never able to "let down their hair" and have fun. Thus, a balance between the three ego states makes for a healthy person.

Life Position

In the process of growing up, people make basic assumptions about their own self-worth, as well as about the worth of significant people in their environment, that may or may not be generalized to other people later in life. Harris[7] calls the combination of an assumption about oneself and another person a *life position*. Life positions tend to be more permanent than ego states. They are learned throughout life by way of reinforcements for, and responses to, expressed needs. These assumptions are described in terms of "okayness." Thus, individuals assume that they are either OK or not OK, or that as people they do or do not possess value or worth. Further, other individuals are assumed to be either OK or not OK.

Four possible relationships result from these life positions: (1) neither person has value ("I'm not OK, you're not OK"); (2) you have value, but I do not have value ("I'm not OK, you're OK"); (3) I have value, but you do not ("I'm OK, you're not OK"); and (4) we both have value ("I'm OK, you're OK").

"I'm not OK, you're not OK" parents and children tend to feel bad about themselves and see the whole world as miserable. People with this life position usually give up. They don't trust other people and have no confidence in themselves.

People with an *"I'm not OK, you're OK"* life position often come from their Compliant CHILD ego state. They feel that others are more capable and generally have fewer problems than they themselves do. They tend to think that they always get "the short end of the stick." This is the most common life position for youngsters because, as "little people," they see their world as "I'm small. I don't have much power, but other people, those big people in my world, seem to have all the power and the rewards and punishments."

People who feel *"I'm OK, you're not OK"* tend to be down on other people for at least two reasons. First, they often regard other people as sources of criticism. They feel that if they're not exactly perfect or right, people will be excessively critical of them. Second, they may want to break away from their father or mother figure (or other authority figure) and become more independent, but they're either not sure how to go about this or they have had unpleasant experiences in attempting to do it in the past.

This is a life position in which the person has had a few "zaps" along the road and feels "I've got a lot of self-confidence and autonomy but I sure don't want to be open, honest, and sharing with others in my environment or I'll get punished." With this life position, listening often tends to stop even when someone is still trying to communicate with this person.

"*I'm OK, you're OK*" is suggested as the "healthy" life position. People with these feelings express confidence in themselves as well as trust and confidence in other people in their environment. Their behavior tends to come from their Nurturing PARENT, ADULT, and Happy CHILD ego states, while seldom being evoked from their Destructive CHILD or Critical PARENT.

Transactions Between Parents and Children

TA may be used to explain why people behave in specific patterns, patterns that frequently seem to be repeated throughout their lives. In TA the basic observational unit is called a *transaction*. Transactions are exchanges between people. The purpose of analyzing the transactional units is to discover which part of each person's PARENT, ADULT, or CHILD is originating each stimulus and response. This analysis enables us as parents to identify patterns of transactions between ourselves and our children. Ultimately this can help us determine which ego state is most heavily influencing our behavior and the behavior of each of our children.

Two types of transactions will be useful for us to know, *complementary* and *crossed*.[8] There are many combinations of complementary transactions; however, the basic principle to remember is that the ego state that is addressed is the one that responds. When this occurs, communications can continue. Complementary transactions are ADULT to ADULT, CHILD to CHILD, PARENT to CHILD, and PARENT to PARENT. Not all complementary transactions are beneficial. What we want to strive for in our relationships are OK complementary transactions — Happy CHILD to Happy CHILD, Nurturing

PARENT to Happy CHILD, ADULT to ADULT, and Nurturing PARENT to Nurturing PARENT. Not-OK complementary transactions involve any of the less healthy ego states. like Critical PARENT, Rebellious CHILD, or Compliant CHILD (when complying does not make sense to the child's ADULT).

Examples of both OK and not-OK complementary transactions are shown in Figure 3. As illustrated in Transaction 1, if a father makes a statement to his son from his Nurturing PARENT, "I want you to stop playing in the street because of all the traffic" and his son responds from his Compliant CHILD, "OK, Dad, I didn't notice all the cars," then we have a completed communication in which information has been easily shared and everyone still feels OK about themselves. If, however, as illustrated in Transaction 2, this father was coming from his Critical PARENT and said something like, "Get out of the street, dummy! You're stupid enough to run into a car" and his son responded from his Compliant CHILD back to his dad's Critical PARENT by getting out of the street, we have a completed communication in which information is shared with a minimum effort, but the son feels "put down" by his father and not OK.

A crossed transaction occurs when a person responds with an ego state different from the one the other person was addressing. When that occurs, sharing and listening stop, at least temporarily. For example, if Alan asks his father a question from his ADULT

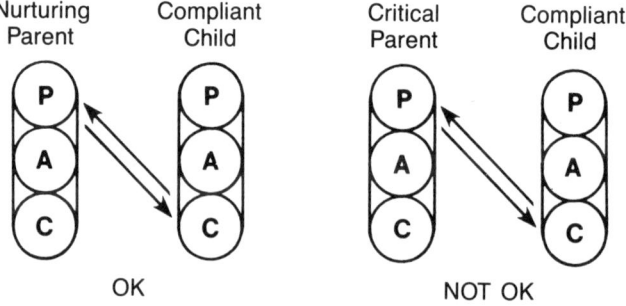

Figure 3. Two types of complementary transactions.

ego state like "What time is it, Dad?" he would expect his father to respond from his ADULT ego state and share information with him, that is, tell him what time it is. If, however, his father responds from his Critical PARENT and answers, "Don't ask so many questions," then a crossed transaction has taken place.

Crossed transactions can either be helpful or destructive to the development of children. The preceding example is a destructive transaction because the Critical PARENT response to Alan's ADULT question leaves Alan with not-OK feelings. Destructive crossed transactions occur between parents and children when either responds to the other from the Critical PARENT or the Rebellious or Compliant Destructive CHILD.

When parents and children fight, a destructive crossed transaction is usually involved. For example, if a mother makes a statement in a Critical PARENT manner ("I don't think you should hang around that girl — she's a bad influence") directed toward her daughter's Compliant (Happy) CHILD and her daughter responds from her Rebellious (Destructive) CHILD ("You have no right to tell me who I can have as friends") to her mother's CHILD, the lines of communication get crossed and the mother and daughter stop listening (although talking or yelling may continue). Now the interaction becomes a win-lose power struggle. Mother and daughter seem to be talking past each other, each matching her "oughts and shoulds" with the other's "oughts and shoulds." If, in this example, the mother wins — and mothers and fathers usually do — the win has a cost. It forces the youngster to Destructive (Compliant) CHILD and teaches her to either "go underground" with her feelings in the future, plot how to get out from under her mother's thumb, or become compliant and do what others say because "I'm not OK."

In some situations, we may find crossed transactions useful in helping our kids to switch out of the less healthy Rebellious CHILD, Compliant CHILD, and Critical PARENT ego states into their ADULT, Nurturing PARENT, or Happy CHILD. This will become clearer as we integrate concepts from TA with Situational Leadership.

Transactional Analysis and Situational Leadership

Being able to respond appropriately to our children when their behavior is being evoked from less healthy ego states and getting them back "on the track" is one of the things Situational Leadership is all about. The key to effective use of a framework like Situational Leadership is to keep our ADULT ego state in the "executive position." When this occurs, we are always diagnosing situations, analyzing alternatives, and weighing the various values before we intervene. When this kind of decision making and problem solving takes place, our emotions and values are under control and we can rationally provide direction and supervision, nurturing and support, or some combination of the two. In other words, we can use any of the four basic leadership styles associated with Situational Leadership. However, when we let our PARENT or CHILD ego states dominate our actions, such flexibility is not often available to us.

People who let their emotional CHILD ego state take control tend to try to influence others only through "telling" (S1) or "delegating" (S4) behaviors. They either want things their way or they retreat into avoidance behavior and don't care about influencing anybody. People who are dominated by their PARENT ego state, whether it be Critical or Nurturing PARENT, seem to be limited to "telling" (S1) or "selling" (S2) behavior. Thus, we feel that parents who diagnose situations before they act, and therefore have their ADULT ego state in control, can be effective more often — that is, provide the right leadership styles at the right times. Applying the appropriate leadership style can have a significant influence on the mix of PARENT, ADULT, and CHILD ego states our children develop, as well as on their life position (attitudes toward themselves and others). As illustrated in Figure 4, these concepts from TA can be integrated into Situational Leadership and can be used as another crosscheck for the maturity judgments we make about our children.

Ego States and Situational Leadership

In terms of Situational Leadership, we would associate Destructive CHILD with low maturity (M1). Therefore, the appropriate

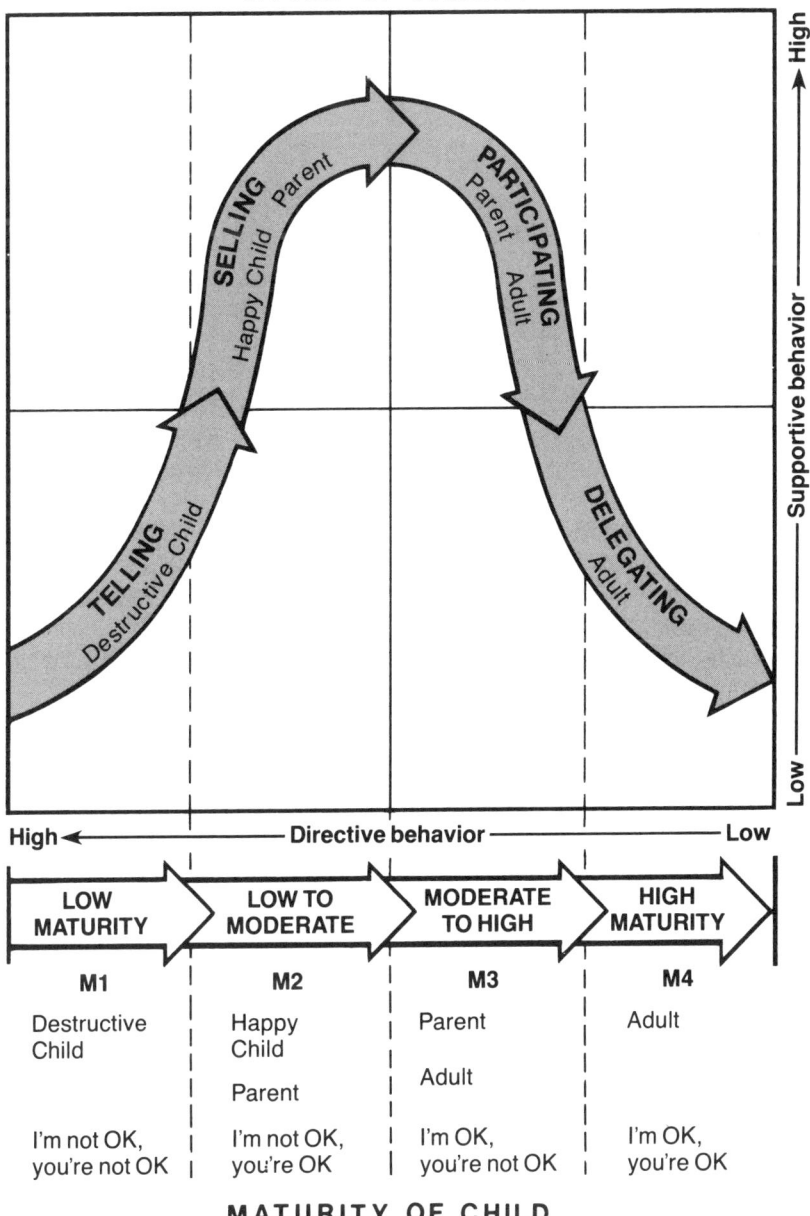

Figure 4. Relationship between Situational Leadership and Transactional Analysis.

leadership style to use with this ego state is a "telling" style (S1). Low positive strokes are appropriate because too much supportive behavior along with the high direction may be viewed as permissiveness and rewarding for inappropriate behavior. Staying in a "telling" style all the time with children in Destructive CHILD, though, is not a good idea. Instead, look for the first sign of positive or constructive behavior, then move to a more supportive "selling" style (S2) and start the developmental cycle. Staying firmly in a very directive style could have some very negative results. Our children are likely to develop their Destructive CHILD ego states even more and may become dominated by either their Rebellious CHILD (no respect for any authority) or their Compliant CHILD ("buckles under" to any authority).

If we are interacting with a Happy CHILD, movement is from low to moderate maturity (M2). Therefore, children operating from this ego state tend to be influenced most readily by a "selling" (S2) style. Since Happy CHILD is not a destructive ego state, two-way communication and supportive behavior should be given along with moderate amounts of what to do, where to do it, and how to do it. The supportive behavior is important because if we treat a Happy CHILD as if he or she were a Destructive CHILD, the consequence is often a self-fulfilling prophecy — the child quickly becomes a Destructive CHILD.

Nurturing PARENT seems to be associated with low to moderate maturity (M2). Therefore, a "selling" leadership style seems to be most effective in influencing children whose behavior comes from this ego state. Any role defining or "telling" what, when, where, and how to do things has to be done in a supportive way. Too much directive behavior without corresponding supportive behavior could convey to children in their Nurturing PARENT that we don't think much of them (they are "not OK" from our standpoint), and they might move to less healthy ego states, like Critical PARENT and Rebellious or Compliant CHILD — particularly if we stay at "selling" too long.

The Critical PARENT ego state generally is associated with moderate to high maturity (M3). Thus a "participating" style

(S3) tends to work best as an initial intervention with children behaving from their Critical PARENT. If we try to use a directive style with these children when they are being very critical and evaluative, it just tends to evoke more Critical PARENT "tapes," and soon we are likely to find ourselves in a win-lose, PARENT-PARENT power struggle with them. To influence children in their Critical PARENT ego state, therefore, we must first convince them that we are supportive and not critical of them. After this initial step, we can be more directive and move to "selling" or "telling" them something.

When our children are operating from their ADULT ego state, we can use a "participating" style or, better yet, leave them alone (S4). Since they are already thinking in rational, problem-solving ways, little directive or supportive behavior is needed as long as they are willing and able to do what they need to do.

Life Positions and Situational Leadership

As illustrated in Figure 4, parents need to direct and closely supervise children whose life position is "I'm not OK, you're not OK." Such children could become destructive to themselves as well as to others. Children stuck at "I'm not OK, you're not OK" may need counseling, therapy, or even institutionalization. Should our children start operating from this negative life position, to get them back on track we need to provide high directive/low supportive behavior (S1) while looking carefully for something positive we can reinforce. This second step is crucial. Too many parents are blind to "good" behavior while on the alert for the "bad." Thus, children with an "I'm not OK, you're not OK" life position first need to be closely directed and then strongly supported for any signs of progress they show. Short-term bursts of "telling" (S1) followed by a "leave alone" (S4) style and then another short-term burst of "telling" only reinforces this potentially tragic life position.

Children who feel "I'm not OK, you're OK" are related to a low to moderate maturity level (M2) and thus need both direction and support. They appreciate direction from their parents because they think their parents are "OK," but they also need supportive behavior to increase their OK feelings about themselves. Children should not be permitted to stay in this life position too long. If our child is in this position, we need to start looking for times when we can delegate more direction, so that he or she can begin to develop some feelings of self-confidence. If this delegation is followed by positive strokes to reinforce progress, we can help our child move through the "I'm OK, you're not OK" life position almost instantaneously on the way to the most healthy life position, "I'm OK, you're OK."

Often parents jump too quickly from "selling" to "delegating," and when their children begin to make mistakes, they move right back to "telling" and "zap" them. When the parents were using a supportive (S2) style, the children were beginning to develop confidence and OK feelings about themselves. Now, when they get "zapped," they either move back to "I'm not OK, you're not OK" (their confidence in their parents and themselves is shaken) or to "I'm OK, you're not OK" (their confidence in themselves survives, but they don't trust their parents anymore). If children get hooked on an "I'm OK, you're not OK" life position, they can develop real problems. In fact, Berne argues that this is often the life position of mentally disturbed criminals, particularly if they were beaten or abused as kids. Since they have been continually "zapped" by their parents or buddies, they have no confidence in others. If we detect any signs of this "I'm OK, you're not OK" life position in our children, we should approach them with high supportive/low directive behavior, so that they will begin to feel OK about us and will be more receptive to increases in directive behavior, if necessary.

Children with life positions of "I'm OK, you're OK" seem to relate to a high maturity level (M4) because they can take on responsibility and can be left alone to carry it out. They feel good about themselves and their parents. They tend to see being left alone as a reward rather than a punishment.

The Problem-Solving Games Parents and Children Play

In the beginning of this chapter we discussed problem ownership and monkey business, and then we moved to TA and the interaction patterns that develop between parents and children. How does all this fit together? The key is problem solving — or the care and feeding of monkeys. If we are going to help our children grow and develop into mature self-motivated individuals, we must gradually let them think for themselves and solve their own problems. Many parents have trouble dealing with their children when they have a problem.

Inappropriate Responses to Children with a Monkey

In TA, a concept known as the Karpman Triangle[9] is helpful in recognizing some dysfunctional reactions when a child has a problem. As Figure 5 indicates, there are three basic roles in the Triangle: Victim, Persecutor, and Rescuer.

Adapting Karpman's concept to problem solving in child rearing, the Victim would be a child with a monkey. A parent could respond to a monkey on a child's back from either the Persecutor or the Rescuer role. If a parent responds from the Persecutor role, the parent puts the child down for having a problem. For example, a teenager, Brooks, might tell his father that he is not getting along lately with his best friend, Ted, and his father may respond by saying, "That's ridiculous! You and Ted have been friends for years. You've never fought before and I can't believe you are having trouble getting along now."

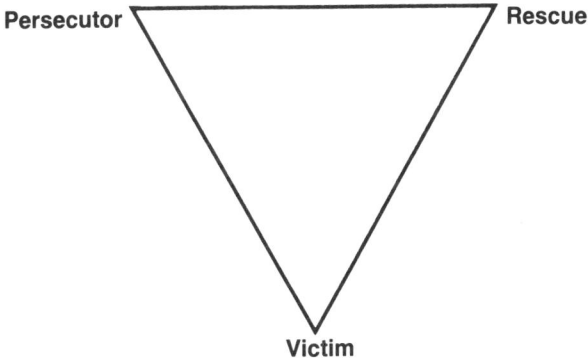

Figure 5. The Karpman Triangle.

The father doesn't even want to recognize that a problem exists for his son.

If a parent responds from the Rescuer role, the parent tries to solve the problem for the child. In our example with Brooks and Ted, the father may respond by saying, "That's too bad, Brooks. Why don't you call Ted and ask him to come over tonight and maybe the three of us could talk this out. I was always able to iron things out with my friends and I'd be happy to talk with you and Ted." In TA and Situational Leadership terms, the Persecutor usually is coming from a Critical PARENT ego state with a "telling" leadership style, and the Rescuer is coming from the Nurturing PARENT and a "selling" (S2) style. The Persecutor denies that the monkey exists and tells the child to forget it, while the Rescuer takes the monkey on his or her back and tends to let the Victim (the child with the monkey) "off the hook." Neither of these responses teaches children to solve their own problems.

The Triangle gets really interesting when a drama develops and people start to change roles. In our example of Brooks and Ted, if the father responds to Brooks's problem with Ted from the Persecutor role and puts Brooks down for having a problem, and if Brooks does a good job as the Victim (mumbles to himself about Ted, looks downcast and thoroughly victimized), his father may begin to feel guilty and realize that maybe Brooks really has a monkey. When that happens, the father usually moves from the Persecutor role to the Rescuer role and attempts to rescue the Victim (Brooks, in this case) — and take the monkey on his back. "I'm sorry, Brooks, for yelling at you. I didn't realize how serious your disagreements with Ted were to you. Maybe I can help out."

At this point, the plot can thicken (as it often does) if Brooks moves quickly from Victim to Persecutor and attacks his father (now the Rescuer) for not being more understanding earlier. "Dad, you never listen to me when I try to tell you something. All I want from you is support, but you always jump to your own conclusions and start yelling." Now the Persecutor turned Rescuer (Brooks's father) is the new Victim.

The drama can also start when the parent initially tries to rescue the Victim — the child with a monkey. What we often find is that most victims don't really want to be rescued. Either they want support, or they only want to complain. So when the rescuing parent starts to make suggestions, the victimized child "yes buts" every suggestion. "Sounds like a good idea having Ted over tonight, Dad, *but* he has a basketball game." Finally when the rescuing parent runs out of good suggestions (that the child didn't want to use anyway), the child moves quickly from Victim to Persecutor and "pounds" his or her parent for not being more helpful. "I thought you said you were good at working things out with your friends. Not one of your solutions will work with Ted and me." So, once again, the parent ends up as the Victim.

The drama gets even more exciting when there are three actors rather than two. This situation usually unfolds when one parent responds to the child with a monkey from either the Persecutor or Rescuer role and the other parent plays the unfilled role. Suppose that when Brooks's dad is persecuting him for having a problem with Ted, his mother jumps in to rescue Brooks. "Don't be so hard on Brooks. His friendship with Ted is very important to him." The rescue attempt makes his father angry and thus he stops persecuting Brooks and attacks Brooks's mother as if she were the Victim. "Why don't you stay out of this? It's between Brooks and me." When that happens, the child escapes unharmed and the parents battle it out.

The drama does not always start with the child as the Victim. Sometimes the child starts off persecuting one of his or her parents. James and Jongeward give a beautiful example of this and how everyone switches roles in their outstanding book *Born to Win*.[10]

Son: (as Persecutor, yells angrily at mother)	*You know I hate blue. Here you went and bought me another blue shirt!*
Mother: (as Victim)	*I never do anything right as far as you're concerned.*

Father: (rescues mother, persecutes son)	Don't you dare yell at your mother like that, young man. Go to your room and no dinner!
Son: (now as Victim sulking in his room)	They tell me to be honest, and when I tell them what I don't like, they put me down. How can you satisfy people like that?
Mother: (now Rescuer, sneaks him a tray of food)	Now don't tell your father. We shouldn't get so upset over a shirt.
Mother: (returning to father as Persecutor)	John, you're so tough with our son. I'll bet he's sitting in his room right now hating you.
Father: (as Victim)	Gee, honey, I was only trying to help you, and you kick me where it hurts the most.
Son: (calling out as Rescuer)	Hey, Mom, lay off, will ya? Dad's just tired.

How can we as parents stop games like this and the drama of the Triangle? As we discussed earlier, parents are best able to use theories and concepts when they have their ADULT ego state in the executive position — that is, when they are able to think before they act.

The way to avoid the role of Persecutor is to listen to our children before we begin to evaluate what they are saying. Active listening helps us gather information so our intervention will be effective, and it helps our children begin to identify and solve their own problems. How about the Rescuer? How do we avoid playing that role?

Keep the Monkey Where it Belongs

William Oncken, Jr., who developed the monkey-on-the-back analogy, warns us not to take on other people's monkeys.[11] In terms of the TA Triangle and child rearing, rescuing is letting a monkey jump from our child's back onto our own back. For example, suppose that our son comes home and says that he has made the club junior tennis team but they have practices on Tuesdays and Thursdays at 3:30 and he doesn't know how he will get there. Most parents would immediately say, "I think I can drive you." If, however, they normally have something planned on Tuesday and Thursday afternoons and cannot make an immediate commitment, they might tell their son, "I'll try to work something out."

Now let's analyze what has just happened. Before the son entered the house, on whose back was the monkey (how he was going to get to tennis practice)? The child's. After he and his mother talked about it, on whose back was the monkey? The parent's. Now who is in the superior position? The child. And in case the parent forgets who's in charge, the child periodically checks in to see how the parent is doing in terms of rearranging his or her Tuesday and Thursday afternoons. In essence, the parent is working for the child. That's what often happens in child rearing. Parents are exhausted from carting their kids all over town, not to mention solving their other problems. This all occurs as if parents did not have lives of their own. Child-imposed time begins the moment a monkey sucessfully executes a leap from the back of the child to the back of the child's parent and does not end until the monkey is returned to its proper owner for care and feeding.[12]

What parents need to do is get rid of their children's monkeys as the children begin to mature. The first step, as we suggested in the beginning of this chapter, is for the parents to determine who owns the monkey. Let's look again at the four problem situations.

1. If our child's behavior is unacceptable but is only a problem to us, then we own the monkey and should do the initial care and feeding. But once everyone knows the monkey

exists, the child should take over its care and feeding. Staying with a "telling" (S1) style will guarantee only that the monkey will stay on the parent's back.
2. If our child's behavior is unacceptable and a problem to both us and the child, then the monkey is astride all our backs. While the child needs some direction on how to feed this monkey, we want to be careful not to use a "selling" style too long, but as soon as possible get the developmental cycle going and move to a "participating" style in which the monkey and its care and feeding are now on the child's back. A "selling" style (S2) can be a rescuing style, which sometimes is okay in the short run, but it could lead to full-time caring and feeding work if it becomes a permanent status quo.
3. If our child's behavior is acceptable to us but is a problem to the child, we should only be supportive of the child's efforts to solve his or her own problem. Be careful in this process that the monkey does not leap onto our back. Be supportive but do not rescue the child and take over the care and feeding of the child's monkey.
4. If our child's behavior is acceptable and neither we nor our child owns a problem, then no parental intervention is needed (use of a "delegating" style), since there is no monkey in need of care and feeding. Some of us get nervous, however, when everything is going well with our children and start "hunting down monkeys and feeding them on a catch-as-catch-can basis."[13] This seems like a useless activity that may grow large monkeys where none really existed before.

It has been our hope in this chapter to help parents realize why it is important for them to eventually work their way out of their traditional job of directing, controlling, and supervising their children's behavior, so that their children can learn to stand on their own feet and be effective in a world that is full of monkeys.

7 • Parents Through the Looking Glass

In Chapter 1 you had an opportunity to complete the PARENT-Self.[1] Now that you've acquired a general framework to help you understand and interpret your responses to that questionnaire, you're ready to score your PARENT-Self answers. Together we will try to find out whether you think you have the ability as a parent to diagnose child-rearing situations and use the appropriate styles of leadership to maximize your impact on your children. You should learn the following:

1. Your perception of your basic leadership style
2. Your perception of your flexibility — your ability to use a variety of styles
3. Your diagnostic skills or adaptability — your ability to use the right style at the right time
4. What your leadership style means in terms of the kinds of situations it is most effective in.

The PARENT-Self

The PARENT-Self was designed to measure three aspects of parent behavior: (1) leadership style, (2) style range, and (3) style adaptability. It's important to remember that the questionnaire you completed measures only *your self-perception* of how you behave as a parent. Thus, it may or may not reflect your actual leadership style, depending on how accurate your perceptions are.

ALTERNATIVE ACTIONS
(Style Range)

SITUATIONS	(1)	(2)	(3)	(4)
1	A	C	B	D
2	D	A	C	B
3	C	A	D	B
4	B	D	A	C
5	C	B	D	A
6	B	D	A	C
7	A	C	B	D
8	C	B	D	A
9	C	B	D	A
10	B	D	A	C
11	A	C	B	D
12	C	A	D	B
Sub-columns	(1)	(2)	(3)	(4)

Figure 1. Determining leadership style and style range.

For this reason, a PARENT-Other questionnaire (see "Bits and Pieces A," following Chapter 8) has also been included in this book to help you find out how your children and other members of your immediate family perceive your leadership style.[2] Comparing the way you perceive yourself with the way other people close to you see you can be very useful. We discuss this in more detail in Chapter 8, "Making It Work." Now, if you're ready to begin, grab a pencil and turn back to your responses to the PARENT-Self in Chapter 1.

Determining Parent Style and Style Flexibility

After you have examined the PARENT-Self, take a look at Figure 1. This chart will help you determine your perception of your leadership style and style flexibility or range. To do this, circle the letter of the alternative action you chose for each child-rearing situation of the PARENT-Self, and then total the number of times an action was used in each of the four subcolumns. As you may have guessed by now, subcolumns 1 through 4 represent leadership styles 1 through 4, that is, "telling" through "delegating."

Next, transfer these subcolumn totals to the Situational Leadership Model presented in Figure 2. The subcolumn 1

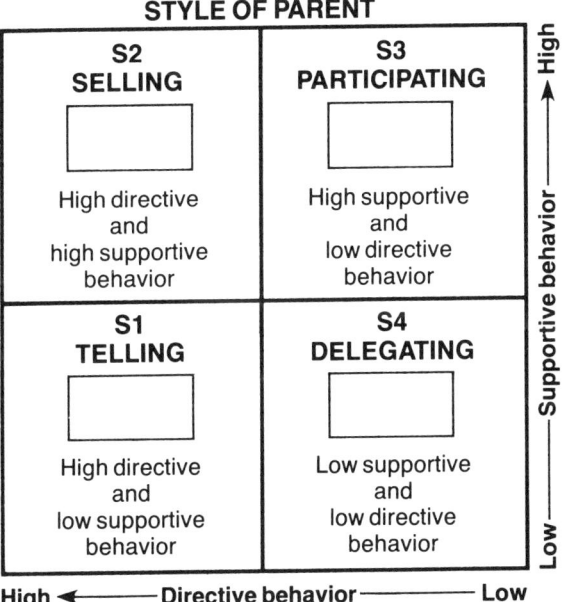

Figure 2. Your parent leadership styles.

total belongs in the Style 1 box (action choices that describe high directive/low supportive "telling" behavior); the subcolumn 2 total goes in the Style 2 box (action choices that describe high directive/high supportive "selling" behavior); the subcolumn 3 total goes in the Style 3 box (action choices that describe high supportive/low directive "participating" behavior); and the subcolumn 4 total belongs in the Style 4 box (action choices that describe low supportive/low directive "delegating" behavior).

Self-Perception of Leadership Style

Now that you have transferred your totals to Figure 2, take a look at it. The way you perceive your leadership style as a parent can be found in the Style of Parent portion of the Situational Leadership Model. Your *primary leadership style* is defined as the style or styles for which you have the most responses. If two or more styles are tied, your primary style includes all of them. In other words, if you had five responses in Style 2 ("selling"), five responses in Style 3 ("participating"), two responses in Style 4 ("delegating"), and no responses in Style 1 ("telling"), your primary style would include Style 2 and Style 3. However, if you had two responses in Style 1 ("telling"), ten responses in Style 2 ("selling"), and no responses in either Style 3 ("participating") or Style 4 ("delegating"), your primary style would be Style 2.

Your *secondary style(s),* that is, the leadership style you tend to use on occasion, is any one or more of the other styles in which you have two or more responses. Therefore, if you had five responses in Style 1, five responses in Style 2, two responses in Style 3, and no responses in Style 4, your primary style would be "telling" and "selling" and your secondary style would be "participating." If, however, you had two responses in Style 1, three responses in Style 2, four responses in Style 3, and three responses in Style 4, your primary style would be "participating," with secondary styles in "telling," "selling," and "delegating." If you had all twelve responses in Style 2 and no responses in any of the other three styles, your primary style would be "selling," with no supporting styles. Therefore, you could have anywhere from zero to three secondary styles, but you will always have at least one primary style.

Style Flexibility

Your *style flexibility* or *style range* is how much you are able to vary your leadership style as a parent. To determine your style flexibility, mark an X under all the parent leadership styles in Figure 3 that you have identified as either primary or secondary. Then place an X opposite "Style Flexibility" for each of those styles marked.

If you have an X under only one style (your primary style) in Figure 3, then you perceive the flexibility or range of your behavior as limited. If you have X's under three or four of the styles, then you perceive yourself as having a wide range of leader behavior. Therefore, if you have an X under only Style 2, then you perceive the range of your behavior as limited to "selling." If, however, you have X's under Styles 1, 2, and 3, then you perceive yourself as being able to use "telling," "selling," and "participating" behaviors.

If you have a wide range of behavior, as determined by Figure 3, you might be "patting yourself on the back," because flexible parents have the *potential* to be effective in a number of child-rearing situations. Before you "break your arm" though, notice that we have italicized the word *potential*. While flexibility can help make you a more effective parent, it has limited value unless you use the right style at the right time. This is where your diagnostic skills or style adaptability come into play.

Parent leadership styles	Style(s)	Flexibility
S1 TELLING		
S2 SELLING		
S3 PARTICIPATING		
S4 DELEGATING		

Figure 3. Parent styles determine style flexibility.

Determining Style Adaptability

Take a look at Figure 4. This chart will help you determine your perception of your style adaptability or effectiveness. To do this, circle the score assigned to each alternative action choice you made on the PARENT-Self (refer to Figure 1), and then total these scores. For example, if you picked action B in Situation 1 of the PARENT-Self, you would now circle the score assigned to that response — in this case, −1.

The weighting from +2 to −2 is based on Situational Leadership. The leader behavior with the highest chance of success of the alternatives offered is always weighted +2. The second best alternative is weighted +1, and the third best is −1. The behavior with the lowest chance of success is always weighted −2.

After you have totaled subcolumns A, B, C, and D in Figure 4, you can determine your total score on style adaptability or effectiveness by adding up each of the subtotals and placing this number in the box marked "Effectiveness." If you had more plus scores than minus scores, your total score will quite obviously be a plus score, and vice versa.

Before we give you any feedback on what your total score means, we'd like to tell you a bit about the design of the questionnaire. This should help you to better understand just what your effectiveness or style adaptability score represents.

Design of the PARENT-Self

The PARENT-Self presented you with twelve situations and four alternative parent behaviors for each. The situations can be differentiated in the following way:

1. Three situations involved low maturity (M1)
2. Three situations involved low to moderate maturity (M2)
3. Three situations involved moderate to high maturity (M3)
4. Three situations involved high maturity (M4).

For each of the situations you were asked to choose from among four alternative actions: a high directive/low supportive

Determining Style Adaptability • 153

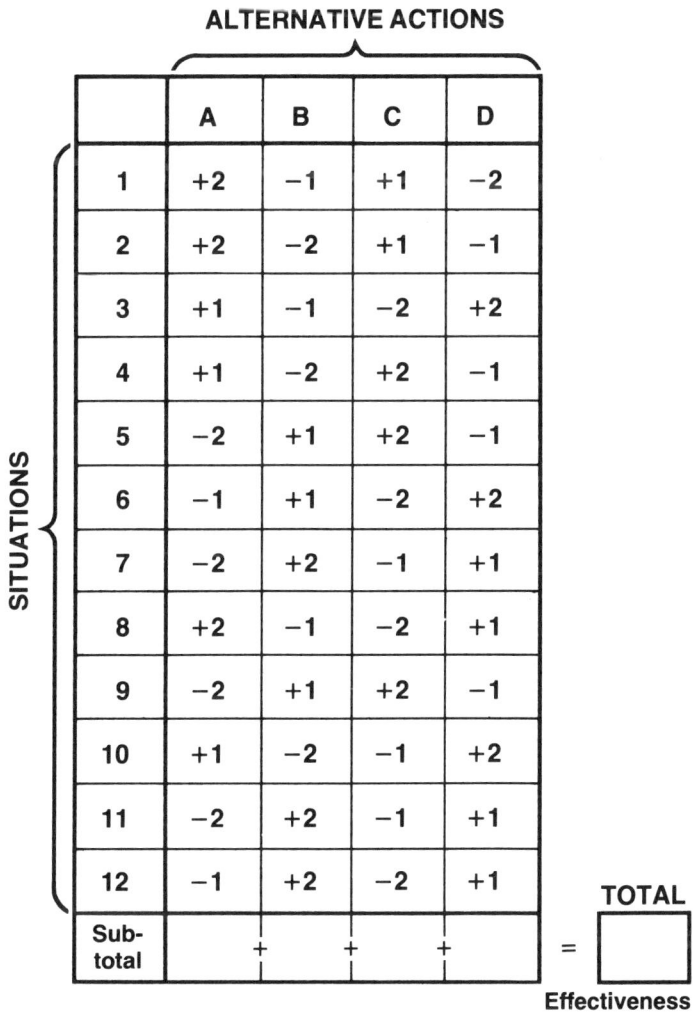

Figure 4. Determining style adaptability.

"telling" behavior (S1), a high directive/high supportive "selling" behavior (S2), a high supportive/low directive "participating" behavior (S3), and a low supportive/low directive "delegating" behavior (S4).

Therefore, if you had selected the parent behavior with the highest probability ("best" chance) of success every time (the +2 choice), you would have scored +24 on the effectiveness dimension.

It is important to note that you could have picked three alternative choices in each of the four styles and yet have had a score considerably less than +24. (We have seen a number of such profiles.) This would indicate that you have a wide range of behavior or flexibility, but the styles are not being used as appropriately as they might be. You need to work on your diagnostic skills — you are "off base."

Perhaps the least significant piece of information given to you is the total effectiveness score you marked in Figure 4. That score does not necessarily indicate how effective you are as a parent. Why? Because the PARENT-Self gives you equal opportunities to make decisions about all levels of maturity. And yet, in most homes, at any given time, parents would probably be dealing primarily with one or two levels of maturity rather than equally with all.

Self-Perception of Style Adaptability

The effectiveness score you marked in Figure 4 is your perception of your *style adaptability*. While flexibility indicates how much we can vary our style, adaptability is the extent to which we can vary our style to meet the demands of a given situation. This gives you a good idea of your overall chance of success in all twelve of the situations to which you responded in the PARENT-Self. Parents with little style flexibility can be effective over a long period of time if they remain in situations in which their style is appropriate. Conversely, parents with a wide range of styles may be ineffective if their styles are not well matched with their situations. Thus, flexibility does not guarantee effectiveness, unless we also have good diagnostic skills — that is, the ability to use the right style at the right time.

To help those of you who are interested in improving your diagnostic skills, the twelve situations from the PARENT-Self and their corresponding alternative actions are analyzed in

"Bits and Pieces B." There, the rationale for evaluating and weighing alternatives is briefly explained. The discussion focuses on why various combinations of directive and supportive behaviors are best in certain situations, and it should be useful to you in applying the situational approach in your own family.

What if You Can't Use the Most Appropriate Style?

The concept of adaptability implies that the effective parent is able to use the right style at the right time. What if a parent makes a good diagnosis and then realizes that he or she can't use the "best" style? Is that parent doomed to failure? It's all a matter of degree. Situational Leadership not only suggests the high-probability parent styles for various maturity levels, it also indicates the probability of success of the other styles if a parent is unable to use the "desired" style. The probability of success of each style for the four maturity levels is shown in Figure 5.

Maturity Level	"Best" Parent Style	Second "Best" Style	Third "Best" Style	Least Effective Style
M1 Low	S1 Telling	Selling	Participating	Delegating
M2 Low to Moderate	S2 Selling	Telling or Participating		Delegating
M3 Moderate to High	S3 Participating	Selling or Delegating		Telling
M4 High	S4 Delegating	Participating	Selling	Telling

Figure 5. Matching maturity level with the parent style most likely to work well.

As Figure 5 indicates, the "desired" style always has a second "best" style choice, that is, a style that would be moderately effective if the highest-probability style could not be used. In attempting to influence children at the low to moderate (M2) and moderate to high (M3) maturity levels, you will notice that there are two second "best" style choices. The choice of which of the two styles to use depends on whether the maturity of the child is getting better, indicating that we are involved in a developmental cycle (Chapter 3), or getting worse, revealing that a regressive cycle is occurring (Chapter 5). If the situation is improving, "participating" and "delegating" would be the "best" second choices, but if things are deteriorating, "telling" and "selling" would be the most appropriate backup choices.

Figure 5 also suggests that "telling" and "delegating" are the risky styles because the lowest-probability style is always one of the two styles. However, even though this appears to be true, later in this chapter we will discuss why it is so important for parents to learn to use these styles effectively.

PARENT Profiles

Now that you've gotten some feedback on your PARENT-Self, you may still be asking, "What does it all mean?" In extensive interviews with parents and children, we think we've formulated a pretty good idea of what your PARENT profile represents. Of course, in sharing this information, we are assuming that your self-perception of your leadership style is actually the way you behave in child-rearing situations. But, as we said earlier, this may not be the case.

In this discussion, we are going to be talking about "two-style profiles." A *two-style profile* represents either two primary styles or a primary style and a secondary style.

As feedback is given on the specific two-style profiles, keep in mind your own profile, which you recorded earlier on Figure 2. If you had a one-style profile (you did *not* have two or more responses for any style other than your primary style), then you need to remember that your profile represents only a portion of the two-style profile. If you had a three- or four-style profile (you had a primary style and the same number of responses in two secondary styles or three responses in all four of the styles), you may have to integrate this feedback into several of the two-style profiles.

Profile: "Telling-Participating"

Parents with a majority of responses in the "telling" and "participating" styles and very few responses in the "selling" and "delegating" styles generally view their children in decidedly positive or negative ways. "Telling-participating" parents give their kids either "warm fuzzies" or "cold pricklies." They view some children as basically lazy, unreliable, and irresponsible and believe the only way to get these kids to do anything is to coerce, reward, punish, and closely supervise them. Other children they see as responsible, self-motivated, and in need of only a little parent support.

The "telling-participating" parent is fond of labels: kids are either "good" or "bad," "helpful" or "troublemakers." Their children see them as playing favorites — being supportive with the kids they "like" and being very controlling and restrictive with the kids they "don't like." Such parents have been heard to say, "He's a really good kid — I never have to worry about him," or "Even though she's my daughter, she's a 'bad apple' — I have to watch her all the time."

This style profile can create problems. While the children who constantly receive a supportive "participating" style (S3) may turn out to be good kids with positive feelings about themselves and others, this is not always the case. This style may also produce children who are spoiled, self-centered, and psychologically dependent on their parents, particularly if a "participating" style is used exclusively. However, children who are always directed and closely supervised ("telling") often turn out to be either passive and dependent or rebels who have no respect for authority. Neither of these results is desirable, of course.

Thus, parents with this profile often are not able (much less willing) to develop the potential of children they don't like or trust because they lack the interim "selling" style (S2) needed to help their kids make the move toward greater maturity. They don't seem to recognize that children develop "bit by bit," and thus they either keep their kids locked into immature states or make rebels out of them. Not only does a parent with a "telling-participating" profile often lack the skills for helping children to mature, he or she also frequently encourages regression in development. Children of parents with this profile claim that if there is any change in their parents' style, it usually involves a movement from "participating" (S3) to "telling" (S1). In other words, although it's very difficult for these kids to receive supportive types of behavior from their parents if "telling" has been the norm, it's not difficult to move in the other direction. A few mistakes, a step in the wrong direction, and these parents may put you on the "bad kid" list.

Profile: "Telling-Delegating"

People whose PARENT scores fall mainly in the "telling" and "delegating" styles usually have a basic style of "delegating" (S4) and a supportive style of "telling," (S1). This profile has some similarity to the "telling-participating" profile — that is, people in this profile tend to "sort" their children into categories. In this case, though, the sorting mechanism frequently is in terms of the child's responsibility. The comments these parents make indicate that if their children act responsibly, they will be left alone; but if they are irresponsible, their parents won't hesitate to "ride them" and closely supervise their every move.

The "delegating-telling" profile is all too common. Many of us tend to take our kids for granted and give them free rein until they get into trouble, then we "zap" them. While "delegating-telling" parents are quite capable of making a disciplinary intervention to get a child back on track, they often lack the developmental skills to take children easily from low levels of maturity to higher levels. After a while, of course, these parents succeed only in teaching their kids to avoid the punishment (that is, the parents).

Some children of "delegating-telling" parents do manage

to make it on their own. Their parents, assuming that "telling is learning," leave them to their own devices. If they're "fast learners," they may mature quickly without any parent support. But if they're not, they soon realize that it's dangerous to venture out on their own with a disciplinary "telling" lurking in the wings. They mistrust situations in which they are given responsibility because they know that one mistake will land them in the S1 "jail" again. Thus, the "delegating-telling" style seems to work with children who mature fast, but keeps those who don't learn the rules of the game quickly dependent and insecure for long periods of time.

If you suspect yourself of "delegating-telling" behavior, think about the question we raised earlier: When was the last time you hugged your child? We don't mean just physically, but psychologically as well. As we emphasized in Chapter 3, the key to helping your kids mature is to use supportive behavior at the right times. Children, as well as adults, need positive strokes. And yet, the "delegating-telling" parent seems only to be able to give negative strokes, "cold pricklies" that teach children what not to do but seldom help them learn what to do. To be more effective, a parent with this style profile needs to practice using supportive behaviors at appropriate times.

Profile: "Selling-Participating"

How about parents who place the majority of their responses in the "selling" and "participating" styles? These people seem to do well with children of average maturity, but find it difficult to handle discipline problems and children who are behaving immaturely (M1). Further, they aren't good at delegating responsibility to their more mature children.

"Selling-participating" parents usually say they like the role of parent; they never want to let go of their kids. By never using a "delegating" style (S4), they prevent their children from ever realizing their fullest potential while at home. They also avoid a "telling" style (S1) because it's important to them to be liked by their kids. Their "warm fuzzy" approach to child rearing means they are able to provide only moderate direction and supervision for their children but go "overboard" on friendly, supportive behavior.

The "selling" and "delegating" parent styles are sometimes called the "safe" styles because they can never be that far off base. In contrast, "telling" and "delegating," as Figure 5 suggested, are in some ways the "risky" styles because, if used inappropriately, they can result in real problems.

For example, suppose Beth and Rob Kohler decide to leave their young teenage children alone for the weekend, although they've always had a babysitter in the past, even for much shorter periods of time. Since the Kohlers have chosen to use a "delegating" style (S4) in an area in which their children have not yet demonstrated maturity, they may be in for a rude surprise when they return home.

Children have to learn gradually to take care of themselves without supervision; they usually can't learn it overnight. Thus, Beth and Rob are asking for trouble by not hiring a babysitter. However, suppose the Kohler children have demonstrated mature, responsible behavior for quite some time and have not had a babysitter for several years. If Beth and Rob suddenly decide to hire Mrs. Jones to stay with their children for the weekend (an abrupt shift to a "telling" style), there is a high probability that the kids will resent this action and will give Mrs. Jones a hard time. Rather than involving their children in any aspect of the decision making, the Kohlers simply told them what had been arranged.

We're not suggesting that you not use the risky "telling" and "delegating" styles. If we're going to maximize our effectiveness as parents, we must be willing to take the risk and use these styles when situations demand them. We're only cautioning you to take some extra time ("do more homework") to make sure your diagnostic judgments are on target before you plunge in — not "high risk" but "calculated risk."

Learning to make Style 1 interventions is useful for several reasons. First, they are effective when you are initially encouraging development of maturity in some aspect of your child's life. In other words, "telling" is frequently a good first move. Without a lot of "what to do, where to do, when to do, and how to do," the child will feel very insecure. "Gee, I know Dad wants me to do that, but I sure wish he would tell me how to do it." The first time a child does something, "telling" is not looked at as negative but as helpful. Second, this style is often necessary for making disciplinary interventions. However, it's equally essential to learn to use a "delegating" style if we are interested in helping our kids develop independence and self-motivation. If we hope to get out of the "child-rearing business" someday and stop "owning" all our children's "monkeys," we must begin now to let our kids try their wings and, by doing so, learn a little bit at a time.

In summary, a "selling-participating" style is an excellent profile for working with moderately mature children who need support and some direction. But parents with this profile must also learn to use the "telling" and "delegating" styles for those occasions when their children need either an extra nudge or the chance to go it alone.

Profile: "Telling-Selling"

People whose responses fall primarily in the "telling" and "selling" styles tend to be able to raise and lower their supportive behavior but often feel uncomfortable unless they are calling the shots — that is, unless they are providing the direction and supervision.

"Telling-selling" parents are usually effective with children of low to moderate maturity. This style seems to be especially successful during the early developmental years and is also useful when a disciplinary intervention is needed. The problems come later, when the early dependent years or the disciplinary action is over. Now these parents are unable to move on; they don't know how to delegate more responsibility to their kids and, thus, stymie their growth. It is this profile that most often produces either the rebellious, disrespectful child or the passive, dependent child who won't make a move without some direction from an authority figure. Neither of these ways of coping with life brings much satisfaction. The rebellious child often begins to develop OK feelings about self but hostility toward his or her parents, while the passive dependent child begins to believe that he or she is not OK but parents and other authority figures are OK.

Profile: "Selling-Delegating"

"Selling-delegating" parents usually have a basic style of "selling" (S2) and a supporting style of "delegating" (S4). Such parents don't feel secure in child rearing unless they are providing much of the direction for the family. At the same time, it's important to them to establish a warm family environment characterized by open communication and high supportive behavior. The "selling-delegating" parent generally likes to make decisions and then convince other family members that those decisions are appropriate. Only occasionally do these parents let their kids make decisions on their own. And when they do, these children are often at a loss because they've had so little experience in this area. In other words, "selling-delegating" parents usually make the mistake of moving from "selling" (S2) directly to "delegating" (S4), without ever pausing at "participating" (S3). Let's look at an example.

A father usually works very closely with his son Carl around the house. He tends to call the shots on what, when, where, and how things should be done but is very supportive of Carl's efforts. They have fun working together. Now suppose that Carl's dad gets behind at the office and isn't able to be at home on Saturdays — yet things still need to be done. So, he asks Carl to take over various projects when he's not around. Carl, rather than seeing this as a sign of his dad's trust and respect, feels that he's being taken advantage of by his father. "Why is Dad giving me all this work? What did I do wrong? Maybe he doesn't like me anymore. He sure stays away from here on Saturdays." In other words, the "delegating" is not seen as a reward, but as a punishment.

In our example, if the movement from "selling" to "participating" to "delegating" had been followed, Carl's father would have first patted him on the back and told him what a big help he had been. Then he would have explained about the problems he was having at work and why he wouldn't be around on Saturdays for a while. He would point out to Carl how things still needed to be done around the house and would ask if Carl felt he could handle any of the jobs on his own. Then they would talk about it. By involving his son significantly in the decisions that needed to be made, Carl's dad would be moving into a "participating" style (S3). After Carl had selected some jobs he was interested in doing, his father would say, "I know you can handle these on your own. But if you have any problems, let me know and we'll see what we can work out." Now the movement from "selling" to "delegating" has passed through the supportive "participating" style. As a result, Carl feels good about helping his dad out on his own.

Profile: "Participating-Delegating"

People whose responses fall mainly in the "participating" and "delegating" styles tend to be able to raise and lower their supportive behavior but often feel uncomfortable if they have to initiate structure or provide direction for their children. Thus, while this profile works well with kids of fairly high maturity, it isn't effective with children who are becoming less mature and need a regressive intervention or with young children who have never been any more mature and thus require more direction during the early years.

Parents of mature teenage children or children who are living at college or out on their own often display the "participating-delegating" profile. It also seems to be characteristic of parents who were raised in a very strict family and say, "We don't ever want to put our kids through that kind of treatment." As a result, they overcompensate by refusing to give their children any direction or supervision for fear of making them feel "the way we did as kids."

Single parents also sometimes have a "participating-delegating" profile. Left with the child-rearing responsibilities by an untimely death or a divorce or separation, these individuals feel that a single parent has to be extremely supportive to overcome the fact that the children have only one parent.

This profile can be very effective with children who are generally quite mature and responsible. It can also be quite successful with less mature children if the directive behavior they need has been adequately taken over by others — for example, babysitters, grandparents, or teachers — and the parent does not interfere with these "harder" interventions.

Thus, the main caution for "participating-delegating" parents is to make sure that their children are getting the outside direction or discipline they may need. Otherwise, they might be nurturing a spoiled brat, a child burdened with a distorted image of his or her own importance.

Implications for Growth and Development

It's probably evident to you by now that all the profiles are effective in certain child-rearing situations. Since most of us will be dealing with various maturity levels among our children (or even with a single child), we need to develop the capacity to use any of the four basic styles appropriately in a given situation. Although some parents lack this flexibility, we've found in working with many parents that with some understanding of Situational Leadership, most seem willing and able to expand their versatility. So don't become discouraged. The most important thing here is motivation — we have to want to be better parents. If we do, most of us have the capacity to increase our style range and adaptability, provided we spend some time carefully diagnosing situations and are willing to risk trying a new style if we think the time is right.

We have confidence in your motivation and ability to change. Therefore, in the next chapter, "Making It Work," we'll show you how you and your family can work together to make everyone more effective in your day-to-day interactions.

8 • *Making It Work*

By this time you probably have a pretty fair idea of how you behave as a parent. It's worth reemphasizing, though, that while it's useful for us to have insight about our leadership style, it's more important to know how consistent our own perception is with the perceptions that others may have of our behavior.

We have found that if a parent's self-perception is closely matched to the perceptions of others in the family, particularly the children, it is far more likely that the parent will be effective within that family environment. Thus, although our PARENT-Self scores are interesting in themselves, they become more powerful when combined with perceptions of others closely associated with child rearing in our family. This is where the PARENT-Other questionnaire comes into play. Once we are armed with this dual information, we are in a good position to make some decisive changes in the way we relate to our children.

What Does Our Self-Perception Mean?

As we mature, we develop certain ways of responding to certain situations. As these behavior patterns become more predictable to ourselves and others, we begin to develop our personality. Our total personality consists of all these behavior patterns. Our parental personality is therefore that portion of our total personality that affects the way we attempt to influence our children. Our parental personality includes our self-perception and the perception of others. A useful framework in understanding exactly what the information from our PARENT-Self means is the *Johari Window*.[1] This concept is used by many people to help increase interpersonal awareness.

Johari Window

Are you intrigued by the name Johari Window? It just signifies the first names of the two psychologists who developed the framework? Joe Luft and Harry Ingham. We use the Johari Window to depict the relationship between a parent's self-perception of leadership style and the perception of others — particularly that parent's children.

According to this framework, there are parts of our parental personality that are known to us and parts that are unknown, as well as parts that are known and unknown to our child(ren). The combination of what is known and unknown to a parent and known and unknown to a child makes up that parent's Johari Window, as shown in Figure 1.

The area that is known to both parent and child is called the *public* area. The area that is unknown to the parent but is known to the child is referred to as the *blind* area. It is unknown to the parent either because the child has been unwilling to communicate to the parent about how he or she is coming across (in other words, the impact that the parent is having on the child while trying to influence that child) or because the parent is not able or willing to receive the messages the child is sending.

The area that is known to the parent but is unknown to the child is the *private* area. It may be private because the parent has been unwilling to share any information in this area with the child or other family members; or it may be private because the others are not picking up the clues or information that the parent is sharing.

The last area, unknown to parent and unknown to child, is called the *unknown*. In Freudian psychology this would be

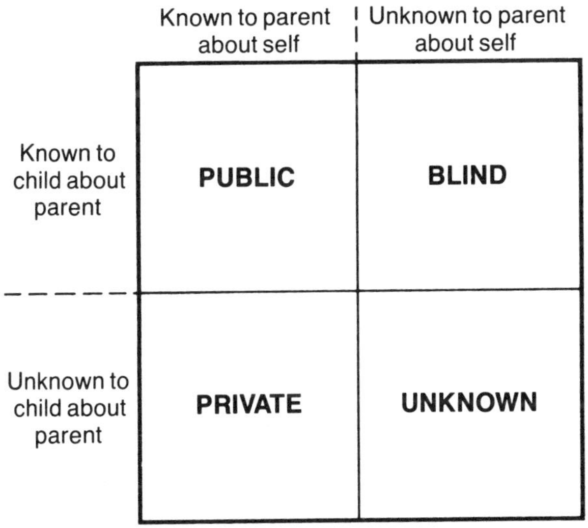

	Known to parent about self	Unknown to parent about self
Known to child about parent	**PUBLIC**	**BLIND**
Unknown to child about parent	**PRIVATE**	**UNKNOWN**

Figure 1. The Johari Window as applied to a parent-child relationship.

referred to as the subconscious or unconscious.[2] Although these attitudes are below the surface, they have an important impact on the way a parent tries to influence the behavior of his or her children.

Feedback

Two processes affect the size and shape of a parent's Johari Window. The first, which operates in the direction shown

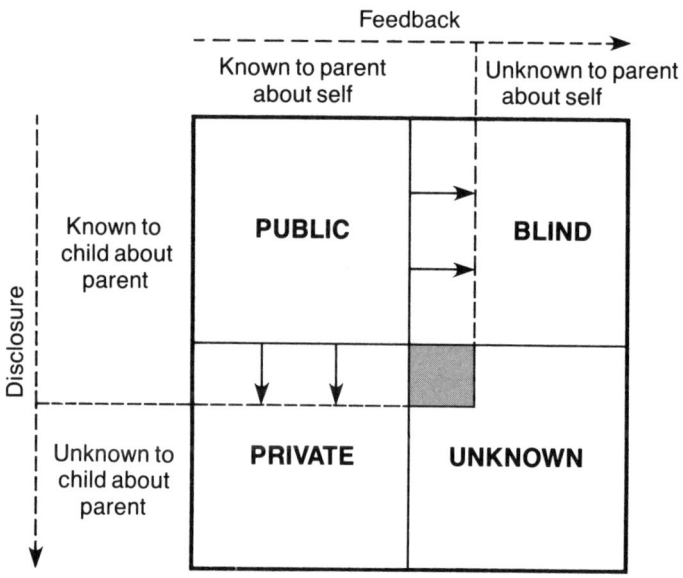

Figure 2. Effect of feedback and disclosure on the Johari Window.

in Figure 2, is called *feedback*. This is communication to a parent that tells the parent how he or she is affecting others in the family. How much feedback a parent gets depends partly on the willingness of family members to be candid and to share relevant information. It also depends, of course, on how much the parent attempts to pick up concerning the perceptions and feelings that are being communicated.

Many parents cut off and eventually stifle feedback from their children by arguing with them about their feelings and perceptions. The late Haim Ginott, author of the well-known book, *Between Parent and Child*,[3] and his wife, Alice Ginott,[4] who has been carrying on some of his work, believe that children should be allowed to have any feeling they want. Feelings are to be heard and accepted; it's only behavior that should be limited. In other words, *everyone* is an expert on their own feelings and perceptions. Parents should never say to their kids, "You don't really feel that way," or "I'm sure you don't see it like that," because obviously their children do know how they feel about things.

To illustrate this point, let's look at an example. A mother is walking through a department store with her young son when the child notices a beautiful bicycle. He says, "Boy, would I like to have a bike like that!" His mother, rather than hearing his feelings, replies harshly, "You're such an ungrateful child. We just got you a new bike for Christmas and already you want a new one. I've had enough of your spoiled attitude. See if you get anything new again for a long time." Now, what exactly has this child learned from this experience? He has learned that he should never tell his mother how he feels about anything; he will only get punished. If this scene is repeated often enough, the mother may soon lose any chance of ever receiving feedback from her son again — which is certainly a high price to pay!

What should the mother do in this situation? Alice Ginott suggests that she should recognize her son's wish and rephrase it in simple words; for example, "I bet you wish you could get a new bike anytime you wanted." The child undoubtedly would agree. Then the mother should follow up with a statement or question like, "Why don't you think you can get that new bike?" The boy knows and will probably say, "Because I just got a new one for Christmas." After agreeing, the mother could conclude the conversation on a supportive note: "When you've gotten good use out of your bike and it starts to get too small for you, then you probably can get a new one." With this kind of interaction, the child won't be afraid to share his feelings with his mother again.

Another suggestion can give us a further clue as to how we can encourage our children to share their feelings and perceptions with us. Why treat our children differently than we would treat a stranger, an acquaintance, or a friend? For example, suppose a guest at a party in our home forgets his hat and we discover it just after he has headed out to his car. Would we run out the door waving the hat and yelling, "How stupid can you be to leave your hat behind? How many times have I had to run after you with something you left? If your head wasn't glued on your shoulders, you'd probably forget that too!" Of course we wouldn't. We'd probably just say, "I'm glad I caught you. You left your hat." And that's how our children deserve to be treated as well.

Treating our children with respect will lead to a relationship in which they feel free to share and talk with us. As we can see in Figure 2, the more feedback a parent gets from a child, the more the public area of the parent begins to displace the blind area. Unless parents receive relevant feedback from their kids, they may become blind-sided — that is, they may discover things their children are doing (like taking drugs) when it's almost too late.

Disclosure

The other process that affects the shape of a parent's Johari Window, as illustrated in Figure 2, is disclosure. This is the extent to which parents are willing to share with children about how they are feeling. Disclosure is more than just words — what people say. In fact, if we are interested in disclosure, we should focus on behavior — what people do. Before we can understand words, we must understand people. It's important to remember that words alone don't mean anything: people give meaning to both words and actions. Therefore, if we want to understand people better and get some real insight into their values and feelings, we have to look at their behavior.

For example, Peggy and Rich Stein are often heard to say, "We're always ready to listen to our kids when they're bothered about something — that's what we're here for." And yet, when friends observe their behavior with their kids, they get an entirely different impression. When John Stein lost a basketball game at school and was feeling down, his parents didn't even give him a chance to air his feelings. Instead, they told him how he should feel: "Now don't be a poor sport, John; you can't always win. We want you to stop this sulking immediately." Or when their daughter, Ann, was upset with a friend, they told her, "Don't worry about Sylvia; we didn't like her anyway. You can do better than friends like Sylvia."

In other words, what the Steins do and what they say they do are two entirely different things. What do you think their kids believe — their words or their behavior? Their behavior, of course! So, after a while, Ann and John will undoubtedly learn to keep their feelings to themselves if they want to avoid a lecture from their parents.

If we, as parents, frequently disclose more information about the way we think or behave, the public area keeps on expanding into the private area, which becomes smaller and smaller, as shown in Figure 2. An interesting phenomenon occurs in families where simultaneous feedback and disclosure is shared between parents and children. Not only does the parents' public area begin to extend into the blind and the private areas, but some of what was previously unknown (not known to anyone in the family) at the subconscious level is likely to be brought into the conscious level and begin to surface in the public area, as depicted in Figure 2.

When we talk about disclosing how we feel to our children, we are not suggesting that we tell all. Rather, we should share only those things that will help our kids understand why we are acting like we are. For example, if we've had a rough day at work, that's important for our children to know — they'll realize that it's not a good time to bug us about doing something. On the other hand, sharing all our anxieties about work might not be the kind of information they need to know.

When the lines of communication stay open and when continual feedback and disclosure occurs, family members not only begin to understand each other better but also learn things about themselves. These insights can help them to interact more successfully with people both inside and outside the home.

Self-Perception versus Style

The PARENT-Self questionnaire, as we explained earlier, reveals only self-perceptions. In terms of the Johari Window, our self-perception would represent what is known to us about our leadership style and would include both our public and private areas. This self-perception of leadership style can be measured by the PARENT-Self. On the other hand, our leadership style (our behavior as seen by our child) would represent what is known to our child and would include on the Johari Window both our public and blind areas. Leadership style in the home can be measured using the PARENT-Other (see "Bits and Pieces A"). The relationship between self-perception, leadership style, and the Johari Window is shown in Figure 3.

One interesting thing we've discovered in our work is that we can predict the shape of the public area through information gathered from the PARENT-Self and the PARENT-Other. For instance, if there is a real difference between self-perception and the way others perceive us, the public area in our leadership Johari Window will tend to be relatively small ("closed"). On the other hand, if there is little difference between self-perception and the perception of others in our family, the public area in our Johari Window will be relatively large ("open"). So, by using the PARENT-Self and the PARENT-Other, we can actually get an idea of the openness of the public portion of our leadership Johari Window in terms of our own perception and the perceptions of various members of the family.

Thus, a father could have his mate, each child, and any other adult involved in child rearing in the family (perhaps a grandparent who is living with the family) complete the PARENT-Other questionnaire on his behavior (directions for the PARENT-Other are available in "Bits and Pieces A" at the end of this book). By comparing his self-perception on the PARENT-Self with the overall PARENT-Other scores from other family members, the father could get a general picture of any discrepancies between how he thinks he behaves in child-rearing situations and how other members of the family think he behaves. In addition, this father could look at the individual PARENT-Self scores from each of his children to find out how the shape of his Johari Window varies from child to child. For example, assume that he has three children: John (age 14), Mary (age 11), and Al (age 9). He may find that he has a very close relationship with John. This might be expected, since they play a lot of golf together and have shared a great deal with one another. There is good feedback and disclosure between them; thus, the father's public window is very open with John. On the other hand, the father spends little time with Mary; he just doesn't seem to know how to relate to her. Thus, the father's public window tends to be closed with

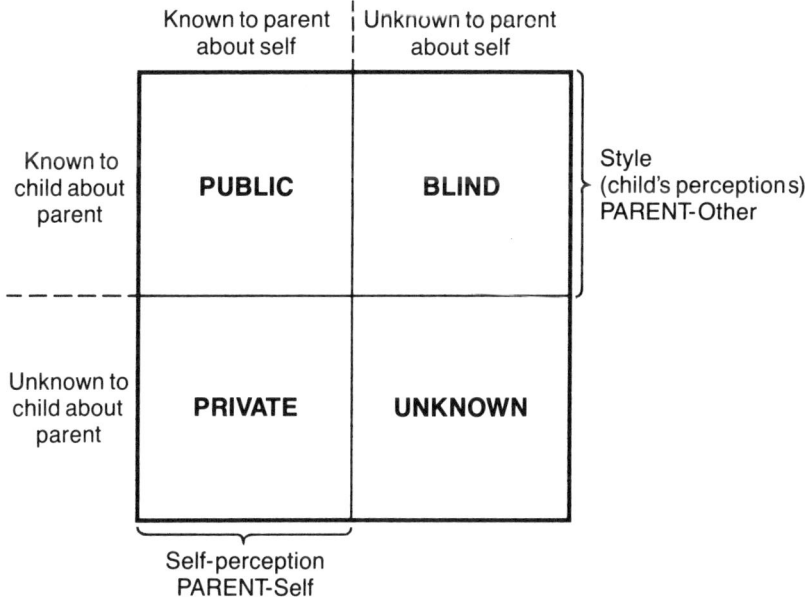

Figure 3. The parent as seen by the parent and the child.

Mary. Finally, the father may have both occasional interaction and moderate rapport (at least more than with Mary) with Al, and, therefore, his public area might be moderate in size.

The Johari Window and Parent Effectiveness

In our work, we have found that the self-perceptions of effective parents are usually right on target. That is, there isn't much difference between how they view their child-rearing efforts and how the rest of the family sees them. Thus, the larger the parent's public area in terms of leadership style (as measured by the *PARENT* questionnaires), the more effective that parent tends to be with his or her children.

Why are parents with "open" public windows more effective

than parents with "closed" public windows? The main reason is that if our public window is open, the communication channels between us and our child are open. Our child is telling us how we're coming across, and we're sharing with our child things that he or she should know. If communication channels are closed between a parent and a child, both have lost their opportunity to influence each other. Let's look at an example.

Harry, a father, has a hard time understanding why he doesn't have more influence on his children. He is a very successful executive; he works hard — nine or ten hours a day and sometimes longer. When he comes home from a long day's work, he's usually so tired that he doesn't want to be bothered by the kids or any problems in the family. He has a "help stamp out kids" attitude. He tells his wife, "Honey, I'm really bushed. Can you keep the kids off my back?" He makes himself a drink and grabs the newspaper. Since he usually gets home about 7:00, the kids often have already eaten dinner, so he doesn't even interact with them at the dinner table. After dinner Harry settles down in front of the TV for the rest of the evening. On weekends, the story isn't much different. Harry usually plays golf and watches sports on TV. Even though the kids are all around him, Harry never seems to get into the act. His communication with them might be described, at best, as "cordial." If Harry's children are bothered by something, do you think they'll go to their father? Of course not. When you have problems do you go to a stranger for help and advice? No. You go to people you know well, people with whom you have an open window.

Then, all of a sudden, Harry wakes up one day to find that he has a teenage son who doesn't have his values, doesn't engage in behavior that he thinks is appropriate. He discovers his son doesn't even want to have much to do with his father. In cases like Harry's, we see a parent who is very effective on the job; there he has an "open" window. But at home his public window is relatively closed because he hasn't recognized that the same things that are important to success on the job (engaging in relevant feedback and disclosure) are the same things that mean success at home. This same thing can happen to a mother if she is so into her job or club duties or housework that she doesn't take time to interact with her kids on a significant basis. The key is not quantity of interaction but quality, uninterrupted time when a parent and child can share feelings and perceptions with each other.

We have seen the opposite too. Some parents are effective at home with their children but don't enjoy the same success at work. They seem to have wide-open public windows at home but "closed" relationships at the office. Yet it is important to develop solid relationships that include relevant feedback and disclosure in any environment where we are interested in influencing the behavior of others.

Keep in mind (in terms of child-rearing) too, that we have separate Johari Windows for the family as a group and for each individual child. Thus, it might be helpful to plan times when we can get together with each of our children separately, as well as with all the children as a family. Many full-time mothers tend to do this intuitively — find opportunities to spend time one-on-one with each of their children.

We might, for example, take each of the kids out for dinner once a month, letting them choose where and what they want to eat. We need to get these sessions on our calendar or our interest in our children may become a matter of attitude, not action. As our children become teenagers we have to check each other's calendars. Often, we cannot talk with our children one-on-one at home. If we sit down alone with a child in his or her room, or our room, the other kids may think we are disciplining the child. Often it is almost impossible to get any one-on-one time with a child in the heart of the house with other siblings, friends, neighbors, the TV, telephone, and even our spouse competing for our attention. In that case, we need to get it on our calendar and get out of the house.

Remember, it's not what we ought to do but what we do that counts. The important thing is to create a situation where the focus is on the child and on opening up the public area between parent and child. We're surprised how willing children are to open up with their parents when no brothers or sisters are around to compete for attention. This process over time will help us develop an open public area with each of our children, as well as within the family as a total unit.

The reason why developing one-on-one relationships with our children is so important is that all of a sudden, when all our kids are no longer kids but adults (they are off in college or in the world of work), our relationship with each of them becomes predominantly one-on-one. Now only on special occasions such as holidays does everyone get together as a group. And on those occasions we usually have other relatives and friends involved. So if we haven't established a good one-on-one relationship with each of our children when they were younger, then we essentially don't have much of a relationship left.

Since we see less of our children as they get older, it is easy to see why, in the midst of all this child-rearing, we should also spend some significant time alone with our husband, wife, or friend. Let's put time with our mate on our calendar too. If we don't have a meaningful relationship with our partner, then when the children are out of the nest and we sit staring at each other across an empty dinner table, the real test of our marriage is about to begin. So let's not give all our energy to our children and not leave anything for each other, because the reality of child-rearing is that eventually all we will have again is each other.

One more suggestion: set aside at least one dinner a week for catching up on what everyone has been doing and what significant things have been happening in the lives of each member of the family. Each of us needs to build opportunities for interacting with the family as a whole as well as for developing openness with individual children and ourselves on a one-to-one basis.

Is It Too Late?

In reading about communication problems, we might be feeling discouraged or even guilty. Maybe we have a problem child or two and are thinking we've really loused up as a parent. Yet, as Wayne Dyer so aptly argues in his book *Your Erroneous Zones*,[5] guilt is a useless feeling.

It is by far the greatest waste of emotional energy. Why? Because, by definition, you are feeling immobilized in the present over something that has already taken place, and no amount of guilt can ever change history.[6]

Today we can never do what we should have done at an earlier time. Wayne brings that point home in a story[7] he tells about when he moved to a new area one February. He called the local electricity company on the Friday he arrived and told them he wanted his electricity turned on. The woman in the service department said, "You should have called on Wednesday." Wayne replied, "Earth to Mars, Earth to Mars...." And she said, "What?" He said, "Is this Mars?" She said "What do you mean?" He said, "I'm on earth and it's Friday and there is no way on Friday I could have done Wednesday, so I thought maybe you were on Mars." She said, "You better speak to my supervisor." When the supervisor came on the line, she told him the same thing, "You should have called on Wednesday." Wayne finally had to go all the way to the president's office to convince them that "on Friday it was impossible to have done Wednesday!"

So, maybe we have made some mistakes. But that was yesterday — now what are we going to do today? Today is the beginning of the rest of our child-rearing days. It's never too late to turn a situation around, as long as we have enough time. We mention time because it's a key factor. Why? Let us try to explain.

The earlier in our child's life we attempt to have an impact, the greater will be our potential influence on his or her future behavior. During the early years, an intervention by us represents a substantial portion of our child's sum experience in that area of his or her life; the same intervention later can never carry the same weight. In addition, the longer behavior is reinforced, the more patterned it becomes and the more difficult it is to change. That's why, as a child gets older, it takes more time and more new experiences to bring about a change in behavior. Think of it this way: one drop of red food coloring in a half-pint bottle of clear liquid may be enough to change drastically the appearance of the total contents. But the same input, a drop of red coloring, in a gallon jug may make little, if any, noticeable difference.

If our children are now teenagers or young adults, it is still possible, though difficult, to bring about some change in their behavior. Now it becomes a matter of economics — how much time we're willing to invest in implementing such a change.

Take our successful executive, Harry, and his teenage son. Suppose the son not only does not have the same values as his father but is into drugs, is in trouble with the law, and has a girlfriend who might be pregnant. What can Harry do now? One choice is to feel guilty and try to make up for past mistakes by putting in all kinds of time with his son now. But his son might resent all this attention from his father when he had been left on his own for so long. If Harry's son doesn't resent the sudden attention from his father, then it becomes an economic question: our children have unlimited needs, but we have limited time. Where can we put in the most effective time with the biggest payoff?

If Harry has plenty of time and decides to attempt to change his son's behavior (even though it's an old pattern), the concepts we've discussed in this book should provide Harry with some helpful clues as to where and how to begin. Probably he will have to do some "telling" (S1) and "selling" (S2) — both of them time-consuming styles. But with some concentrated time, Harry can probably have an impact on his son's behavior.

Before throwing ourselves into a change effort with one of our kids, it's a wise idea to consider what impact this attention will have on other children in the family. By devoting all our time and energy to one problem, we may unwittingly create others. If all of Harry's time is spent on his teenage son, the other children still at home may get the impression that the only way to get time with dad is by getting into trouble (in effect, Harry has put all their good behavior on "extinction"). And soon one problem child has mushroomed into other problem children. So, it's important always to look at the big picture and allot our time accordingly.

The lesson to be learned in Harry's case is to "get our shots in early" with our children. As we stated in our chapter on "Stopping Slippage," giving birth is much easier than resurrection. Rescue and salvage work is tough and time-consuming and often comes too late to do much good.

Team Building in the Family

Parents have to work together as a team in child rearing to ensure that their efforts won't cancel each other out. "Easier said than done," you're probably thinking — and we would have to agree. Coordinating all the various approaches to raising kids that may exist in one household is no easy task.

If the responsibility for child rearing in a family falls on one parent alone, we will have to try to learn, on our own, how to use all four of the basic leadership styles when and if appropriate. (We will talk about that in a while.) In a two-parent or two-adult family where child-rearing responsibilities are somewhat shared, this might not be as necessary if the two adults involved have different style profiles (see Chapter 7). For example, a perfect match would be a "telling-selling" parent with a "participating-delegating" parent. Together, they have all the styles covered.

Of course, parents with two different approaches to child rearing often wind up at each other's throats. They spend hours trying to convince the other parent that they are "right." What we try to make clear to such parents is that, in terms of Situational Leadership, having two different approaches is an asset rather than a liability. In fact, these parents potentially have the capacity to be more effective in a variety of child-rearing situations than parents who think and behave the same way.

What these parents have to do to become a successful team is to make sure of two things. First, they must understand each other's role and style — that is, know when a particular style is appropriate and when it isn't. Thus, if there is a disciplinary intervention that has to be made, the "telling-selling" (S1-S2) parent might be better able to handle the situation in the short run than the "participating-delegating" parent.

If, on the other hand, the children are behaving well and only need support and active listening, then the S3-S4 parent should probably play a dominant role in the short run. We say *in the short run* in these two examples because, eventually, we think both parents, through observing their mate and practicing, have the potential to use the other's "dominant" styles as well. Each will expand his or her own adaptability so that neither parent will become typecast as the "good guy" or "bad guy."

Second, to become an effective team, parents who have different child-rearing approaches must have the same goals. Parents with different child-rearing goals will soon find themselves in the midst of conflict, since they do *not* understand what the other is trying to do. Thus, a key step to effective parenting is to determine with our mate exactly what areas of our children's lives we want to influence. Be specific: tell each other what we think are desirable behaviors in those areas.

Developing Your Style Range and Style Adaptability

As we discussed in the last chapter, *style flexibility* or *style range* is the extent to which we are able to vary our leadership style as a parent, while *style adaptability* is the degree to which we can vary our style to meet the demands of a given situation. If we've caught on to the basic concepts of Situational Leadership, we should by now have a fairly good idea of when to vary our style with our kids. The next thing we have to work on, then, is expanding our style range. Is that possible?

Even if the profile we came up with on the PARENT-Self suggests we tend to be comfortable using only one or two of the four basic leadership styles, we're confident that all of us can expand our style range to meet the demands of the four maturity levels. Expanding our range is particularly crucial in one-parent families, since only one adult is available to raise the children. It's also important in two-parent families, because it's not always convenient or effective to wait to deal with a child until the "right" parent gets home. Both supportive and directive behavior are much more effective the closer they occur to the behavior we want to influence. But how can we learn to use a style that's not comfortable for us?

First, we must "psych ourselves up" – get ourselves mentally ready, as an athlete does when up against a new opponent. One couple we know, where both husband and wife were "participating" (S3) parents, had an interesting strategy. If they found that one of their kids wasn't behaving well and needed a "telling" or "selling" intervention, the parent who got the assignment to intervene would take a walk around the block and get mentally prepared. He or she would even jot down a few notes like, "Now, I'm going to have to do some 'telling,' but I shouldn't be too emotional, because we never really made it clear to Derek what he was to do," or, "I'm going to have to discipline Derek, but I'm not going to blow my cool — I'm just going to tell him what he needs to do to shape up." It's almost like practicing a part in a play. Even if we're not comfortable in the role we're playing, if we're to do a good job, we have to throw ourselves into the role. Often, the styles that parents learn to use (versus their natural styles) are their most effective styles, because they know more about them and use them only consciously and deliberately.

Who Determines Our Parent Style?

When we talk about team building in the family, we don't mean to give the impression that parents are the only members of the team. The sooner we begin to share Situational Leadership with our children — that is, clarify what is expected of them — the sooner the kids can become members of the family team. This means that we no longer are the sole determiner of the style we use with our children. The children now play a vital role. If they have parents who are Situational leaders, they start to realize that it's *their behavior* (not their parents) that determines the leadership style to be used with them. Thus, if everyone in our family knows Situational Leadership, the children (especially teenagers) realize how they can keep us "off their backs." All they have to do is behave in mature, responsible ways, ways that everyone has agreed are appropriate, and we will be supportive (S3) or leave them alone (S4). On the other hand, if they behave immaturely they know we will be "all over them." But now they know why they are getting that kind of treatment from us as parents and how they can get us to treat them in a more supportive way again — by shaping up. We must remember, though, that this is effective only if we as parents are consistent (that is, we treat our children the same way in similar circumstances), even when it is inconvenient and/or makes us unpopular with them.

A father we know told his son that he wanted him to keep his room neat and orderly. If he did, then he wouldn't get hassled. The son, during Little League season, liked to wake his father up about 6:00 in the morning to get in some pitching practice before school. Instinctively, the boy knew he would wish he had never awakened his dad this early if his father happened to find the son's room a mess. His father always responded to a messy room in the same firm, direct way. As a result, what do you think the condition of his room was when he woke his father up? You'd better believe it. Neat!

Thus, Situational Leadership is a vehicle to help parents and children understand and share expectations in the family. If they know what's expected of them, children can gradually learn to supervise their own behavior and become responsible, self-motivated individuals.

Concluding Remarks

The crux of our message in this book is growing okay children who, when they have become adults and made their mark on the world, will say, "I have done it myself." They will no longer depend on their parents for the care and feeding of their "monkeys" (problems). In fact, mature, self-motivated people see the world out there not as full of problems but as full of challenges. Thus, parents are not people to lean on, but people to make leaning unnecessary.[8] Our goal has been to equip all of us with a conceptual framework — Situational Leadership — that can help us apply the conclusions of the behavioral sciences.

Some parents might now be saying, "These theories and concepts are interesting, but they don't account for many of the things that happen in my family." Our response is that if theories and concepts were as complicated as the real world, they would be virtually useless as a sorting device. An analogy might be helpful. Suppose we were drowning in a sea of information. How could we save ourselves? Some might argue that we should drink as much of the information as possible, in the hope that the level of the sea would go down. Yet, with that strategy, the probability is high that we would drown very quickly.

So let's look at it another way. Why doesn't a fish drown when fish are operating constantly in a drowning environment? The reason is that fish have a built-in mechanism that enables them to take from the water what they need and leave what they don't need. It's our hope that some of the concepts and theories presented in this book may become that mechanism for all of us as parents. If that happens, the mechanism will help us sort out what's happening in our family, increase our "behavioral batting average," and, in the process, make us more effective parents.

Good luck!

Bits and Pieces A

PARENT-Other Perception by Others (Parent Leadership Style)

Directions: Assume _____(name of parent)_____ is involved in each of the following twelve child-rearing situations. *Read* each item carefully. Think, about what this parent would do in each circumstance. Then *circle* the letter of the alternative action choice that *you* think would most closely describe the behavior of this parent in the situation presented, based on your experience with him or her. Circle only *one choice.*

Please *do not* respond to the items in terms of what you think a parent ought to do — this is not a test or quiz. Respond to the items according to how you think this parent *has behaved* in the past when you observed him or her in situations similar to those described, or according to how you think this parent *would behave.* (If the situation implies that the parent is married and this parent is a single parent, or if the situation involves a girl and the parent only has boys, etc., answer in terms of how you think the parent would behave.)

Respond to the items sequentially; that is, do item 1 before you do item 2, and so on. Do not spend too much time; respond to each item as if this parent was responding to a real-life situation. Don't go back over the questionnaire; go with your original response.

PARENT-Other

Situation 1

This parent's children are not responding lately to the friendly ways they have been asked to help around the house. Their chores are not getting done and their rooms are a mess.

Alternative Actions

This parent would . . .
A. direct and closely supervise the completion of their chores.
B. in a pleasant and friendly manner, continue to encourage their helping around the house.
C. discuss the situation with the children and then make sure that they complete their chores.
D. not do anything at that time; would assume their behavior will improve.

Situation 2

This parent's children are getting better in doing their homework each evening. The parent has been strict in checking to see that all their assigned work has been done. Reports from school show improvement.

Alternative Actions

This parent would . . .
A. express approval of the results, but continue to make sure the assignments are completed.
B. since they have improved, let them do the work on their own now.
C. express approval and be available for help as needed.
D. continue to direct and supervise their homework.

PARENT-Other (continued)

Situation 3

This parent's children are unable to resolve a conflict with some of their friends. The parent has normally not interfered in these situations. In the past, the children have seemed to take such conflicts in stride and have worked out the problems themselves. This time this approach is not working.

Alternative Actions

This parent would . . .
A. discuss the problem with the children and direct their efforts at problem solving.
B. let them work it out themselves as they have done in the past.
C. tell the children how to solve the conflict and make sure they do it.
D. encourage the children to resolve the conflict and be supportive of their efforts.

Situation 4

This parent is considering some rearranging in a son's room. Lately, the son has demonstrated responsibility around the house and he is presently taking good care of his room. Recently he talked with his parent about changing his room arrangement.

Alternative Actions

This parent would . . .
A. participate with the son in deciding about the rearrangement and be supportive of his efforts.
B. decide what rearranging has to be done and then direct the completion of those changes.
C. allow the son to decide how he would like to alter his room. Let him do it on his own.
D. discuss with the son ideas for rearranging, but make the final decisions on the changes to be made.

PARENT-Other (continued)

Situation 5

The behavior of this parent's daughter has been deteriorating during the last few months. She has been uncooperative and inconsiderate to family members. She has continually needed reminding to do her household chores on time. "Laying down the law" and making sure she is helpful and cooperative have helped in the past.

Alternative Actions

This parent would . . .
A. consider this a stage she is going through and not do anything now.
B. listen to the daughter and find out what she thinks about her behavior, but see that she gets her chores done and shows respect toward family members.
C. act quickly and firmly to correct and redirect her behavior.
D. sit down and discuss the situation with her and find out what she thinks ought to be done; take no direct steps.

Situation 6

This parent has just returned from the hospital where the parent has been recovering from an illness. During the parent's absence the family situation ran smoothly. The spouse at home was closely supervising the children. The parent wants to maintain good behavior, but also wants to get the children involved in family decision-making.

Alternative Actions

This parent would . . .
A. do what can be done to make the children feel important and involved.
B. continue with close supervision and guidance.
C. let the children direct their own behavior.
D. begin to let the children have some role in family decision making, but be careful that decisions made are carried out.

PARENT-Other (continued)

Situation 7.

Due to a parent's new job, work around the house needs to be shared in a different way. The children understand the problem and have made suggestions on how they could help. They have usually done their chores in the past.

Alternative Actions

This parent would . . .
A. tell the children what their new jobs are and then closely supervise the completion of those jobs.
B. participate with the family in deciding new ways to share the expanding responsibilities and support their cooperative efforts.
C. be willing to make new work assignments as recommended by the children, but would make sure that everyone is doing his or her share.
D. just let the assuming of new responsibilities emerge; he or she would take no definite action.

Situation 8

This parent's children are behaving in responsible ways and get along well with each other and their parents. Yet the parent feels somewhat unsure about a lack of direction and supervision of their activities.

Alternative Actions

This parent would . . .
A. stop worrying about it and continue to leave them alone.
B. decide what action to take and then discuss the decision with the children.
C. take steps to direct and supervise their behavior.
D. discuss the situation with the children and reach agreement on an action.

PARENT-Other (continued)

Situation 9

This parent's children are way behind in some fall cleanup they have been asked to do around the outside of the house. Often, they don't show up when they are supposed to work. When they do appear, rather than working, they play and fool around.

Alternative Actions

This parent would . . .
A. let the children continue to set their own work schedule. The parent would assume they know what has to be done and will eventually get around to it.
B. ask the children why the job is not getting done and listen to any suggestions they may have, but supervise the completion of the job.
C. direct and closely supervise the children until the job is done.
D. discuss the situation with the children in a friendly manner.

Situation 10

This parent's son, usually able to take some responsibility for handling money, is not responding to a change in spending, caused by the family's present financial situation.

Alternative Actions

This parent would . . .
A. allow the son involvement in determining the necessary spending limits and be supportive of his suggestions.
B. restate the new limitations to the son and then closely supervise his spending.
C. avoid confrontation by not saying anything about his spending; leave the situation alone and assume it will all work out.
D. discuss the problem with the son and answer questions about the family's money situation, but see that he follows the new plan.

PARENT-Other (continued)

Situation 11

This parent's teenage daughter has been conscientious about doing her homework and helping around the house without supervision. Now that she is beginning to date, she seems to be on the phone much of the time and her schoolwork and chores are suffering.

Alternative Actions

This parent would...
A. restrict her phone calls and supervise the completion of her homework and chores around the house.
B. discuss the new development with the daughter and give her an opportunity to participate in the solving of the problem.
C. discuss the situation with the daughter and get her suggestions; then, develop a plan she will have to follow.
D. not intervene now; see if she realizes the problem and does something to correct it.

Situation 12

Recently, this parent's children seem to be upset with each other. Over the last several years they have gotten along well together. During that period of time, all the children have done extremely well in school and have taken responsibility for their chores around the house. They have worked in harmony together on family projects and have been able to settle any difficulties on their own.

Alternative Actions

This parent would...
A. talk with the children about the situation and then decide alone what needs to be done to remedy it.
B. not interfere; wait to see if the children work it out themselves.
C. act quickly and firmly to correct and redirect.
D. discuss the situation with the children and be supportive.

Scoring the PARENT-Other

Since the situations and alternative action choices in the PARENT-Other are essentially the same as those in the PARENT-Self, the scoring procedure described in Chapter 7 for analyzing the PARENT-Self is also appropriate here. For your convenience in scoring the PARENT-Other, Figures 1–4 from Chapter 7 are repeated here.

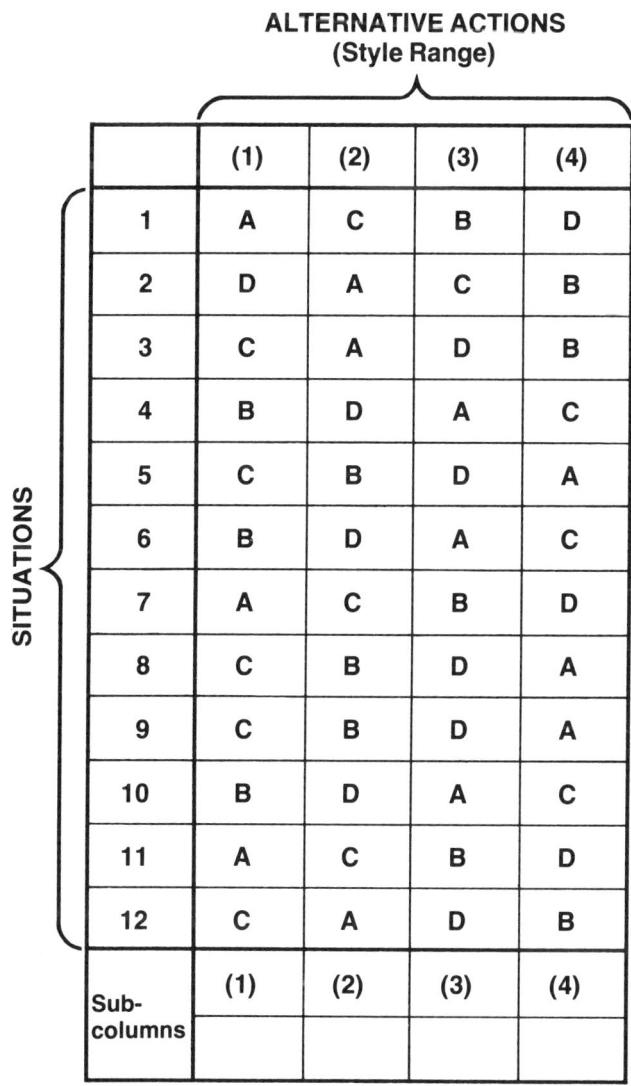

Figure 1. Determining leadership style and style range.

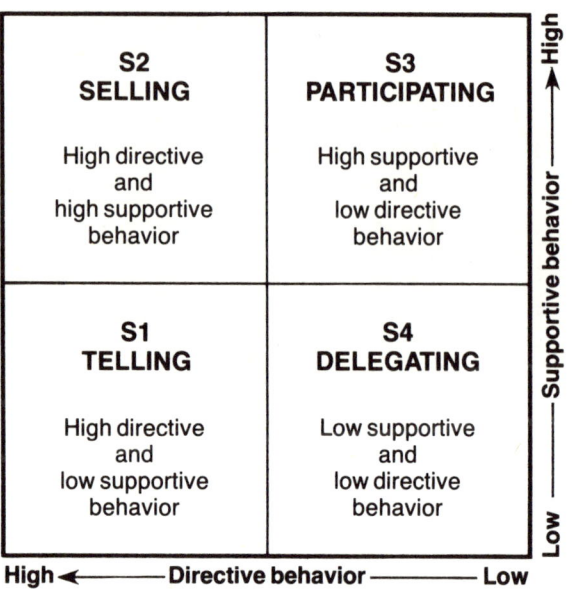

Figure 2. Scoring your basic parent styles.

Parent leadership styles	Style(s)	Flexibility
S1 TELLING		
S2 SELLING		
S3 PARTICIPATING		
S4 DELEGATING		

Figure 3. Parent styles determine style flexibility.

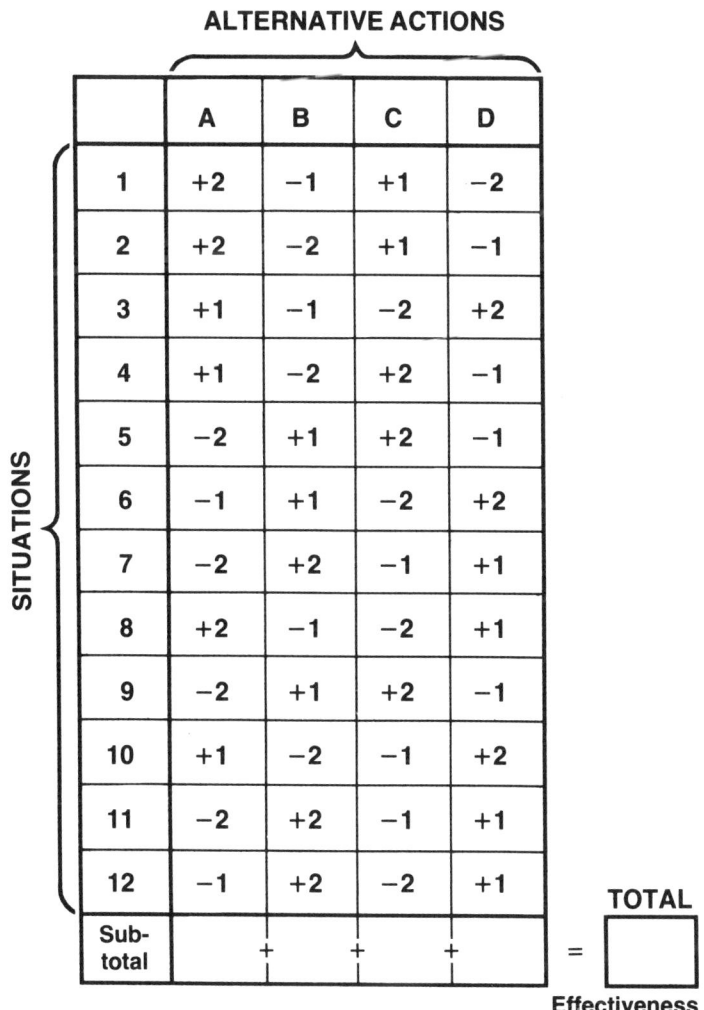

Figure 4. Determining style adaptability.

Bits and Pieces B

Analysis and Rationale for the Twelve Situations from the PARENT-Self

In this section, the twelve situations from the PARENT-Self and their corresponding alternative actions are analyzed, according to Situational Leadership. Since the rationale for and analysis of the PARENT-Self responses are essentially the same for the PARENT-Other, the following situations are written in the third person. For each situation, the alternative actions are listed in order of their effectiveness, not in alphabetical order.

Situation One

The children are not responding lately to the friendly ways their parent has been asking them to help around the house. Their chores are not getting done and their rooms are a mess.

Diagnosis

The children are rapidly decreasing in maturity, as evidenced by the condition of their rooms and the fact that their chores aren't getting done. It is likely that the children now perceive their parent as permissive, because of the high degree of supportive behavior he or she is displaying. The parent's best bet in the short run is to cut back significantly on supportive behavior and increase directive behavior; that is, explain exactly what chores the children are to do and when, where, and how these tasks are to be accomplished. If the children begin to show some signs of assuming responsibility, the parent can begin to increase supportive behavior and again start to delegate. This is an example of the need for a disciplinary intervention in a regressive cycle.

Alternative Actions

The parent would:

A. Direct and closely supervise the completion of their chores.

Rationale: (+2) This action (S1 — high directive "telling" behavior) provides the direction and supervision needed to increase immediately the maturity of the children in this area.

C. Discuss the situation with the children and then make sure that they complete their chores.

Rationale: (+1) This action (S2 — high directive and supportive "selling" behavior) may be appropriate if the children begin to demonstrate some willingness to help around the house.

B. In a pleasant and friendly manner, continue to encourage the help of the children around the house.

Rationale: (−1) This action (S3 — high supportive "participating" behavior) is appropriate for children moderate to high in maturity who are showing ability and willingness to assume some household responsibilities, seeking out the parent only for support and encouragement in special situations. At present, these children are not at that level of maturity.

D. Not do anything now; assume their behavior will improve.

Rationale: (−2) This "hands-off" action (S4 — low supportive and low directive "delegating" behavior) will only increase the probability that this behavior will continue.

Situation Two

The children are getting better in doing their homework each evening. The parent has been strict in checking to see that all their work has been done. Reports from school show improvement.

Diagnosis

The children have been responding well to directive behavior from their parent; their maturity in the homework area seems to be increasing. The parent, although needing to change his or her style to reflect this increased maturity, must be careful not to increase support too rapidly. Too much support and too little direction may be seen by the children as permissiveness. The best bet, therefore, is to positively reinforce gradual improvement (learning "a little bit at a time") as the children's behavior comes closer and closer to the parent's expectations. This calls for a two-step process: first, reduction in directive behavior, and, second, if adequate performance follows, an increase in supportive behavior. These are the correct steps in a developmental cycle.

Alternative Actions

The parent would:

A. Share pleasure with the results, but make sure the assignments are done.

Rationale: (+2) This action (S2 — "selling") will best facilitate increased maturity in this area. While some direction and supervision is maintained by making sure that the children do their assignments, appropriate behavior is positively reinforced through praise and support.

C. Express approval and be available for help as needed.

Rationale: (+1) While the children are maturing in this area, this action (S3 — "participating") might be increasing supportive behavior too rapidly. If the children continue to develop and take more responsibility, this style then would be appropriate.

D. Continue to direct and supervise their homework.

Rationale: (−1) This action (S1 — "telling") reveals no change in leadership style and, as a result, in no way positively reinforces the children's improved performance. With no increase in supportive behavior or opportunity to take more responsibility, the children are likely to level off or decline in this area rather than continue to increase.

B. Since they have improved, let them do the work on their own now.

Rationale: (−2) This action (S4 — "delegating") would turn over too much responsibility to these children too rapidly. Direction and supervision should be cut back gradually, with incremental increases in supportive behavior.

Situation Three

The children are unable to resolve a conflict with some of their friends. The parent has normally not interfered in these situations. In the past, the children have seemed to take such conflicts in stride and have worked out the problems themselves. This time this approach is not working.

Diagnosis

As seen by their ability and willingness to resolve conflicts in the past, the children have been above average in maturity in this area. Now, however, they are unable to resolve a conflict and need an intervention from the parent. The parent's best bet is to move back to Style 3 ("participating") and reopen communication channels by bringing the children together and helping them problem solve. This is an example of a parent moving back appropriately in a regressive cycle.

Alternative Actions

The parent would:

D. Encourage the children to resolve the conflict and be supportive of their efforts.

Rationale: (+2) This action (S3 — "participating") allows the children to come up with their own solution to the conflict, but does not cast them totally adrift. The parent is still available to play some role in the decision-making process if necessary.

A. Discuss the problem with the children and direct their efforts at problem solving.

Rationale: (+1) This action (S2 — "selling") might be appropriate if the children continue to be unable to resolve the conflict.

B. Let the children work it out themselves as they have done in the past.

Rationale: (−1) This action (S4 — "delegating") is no longer appropriate. Since the children have been unable to solve the problem on their own, some help is needed from the parent.

C. Tell the children how to resolve the conflict and make sure they do it.

Rationale: (−2) This action (S1 — "telling") is an overreaction. The children have demonstrated maturity in the past in resolving conflicts and only need some assistance in getting back on track.

Situation Four

The parent is considering some rearranging in a son's room. Lately the son has demonstrated responsibility around the house and he is presently taking good care of his room. Recently he talked with his parent about changing his room arrangement.

Diagnosis

Since the parent is considering some rearranging in the son's room and the child is behaving in mature ways and seems to recognize the need for a change, the parent's best action is to let the son decide and carry out any rearranging himself.

Alternative Actions

The parent would:

C. Allow the son to decide how he would like to alter his room. Let him do it on his own.

Rationale: (+2) This action (S4 — "delegating") would maximize the involvement of this mature child in developing and carrying out any changes in his room.

A. Participate with the son in deciding on the rearrangements and be supportive of his efforts.

Rationale: (+1) This action (S3 — "participating") allows the boy a high degree of involvement in developing the change and may be appropriate if the rearranging means venturing into some unfamiliar areas, like pricing and selecting new carpet, where some help from the parent would be appreciated.

D. Discuss with the son ideas for rearranging, but make the final decisions on the changes to be made.

Rationale: (−1) This behavior (S2 — "selling") would not fully challenge the son's potential nor support his past mature behavior.

B. Decide what rearranging has to be done and then direct the completion of those changes.

Rationale: (−2) This action (S1 — "telling") would be inappropriate with a mature son who has the potential to contribute to the development of any changes in his room.

Situation Five

The behavior of the daughter has been deteriorating during the last few months. She has been uncooperative, and inconsiderate to family members. She has continually needed reminding to do her household chores on time. "Laying down the law" and making sure she is helpful and cooperative have helped in the past.

Diagnosis

The daughter is relatively immature, not only in terms of willingness to take responsibility, but also in her behavior. Closely supervising and directing her efforts has helped in the past. The parent's best bet in the short run is to engage in high directive "telling" behavior (S1) — that is, spelling out her tasks and closely supervising her activities and behavior.

Alternative Actions

The parent would:

C. Act quickly and firmly to correct and redirect her behavior.

   Rationale: (+2) This action (S1 — "telling") provides the directive leadership needed to increase the responsibility and maturity of this child in the short run.

B. Listen to her and find out what she thinks about her behavior, but see that she gets her chores done and shows respect toward family members.

   Rationale: (+1) This action (S2 — "selling") is appropriate for a child of moderate maturity. At present, however, the daughter does not have the motivation or past good behavior to be involved in a discussion of her problem. As she begins to mature, this may become a more appropriate style.

D. Sit down and discuss the situation with the daughter and find out what she thinks ought to be done; take no direct steps.

   Rationale: (−1) This action (S3 — "participating") would tend to reinforce the daughter's present inappropriate behavior. In the future, the parent may find her engaging in other disruptive behavior to gain attention.

A. Consider this a stage the child is going through and not do anything now.

   Rationale: (−2) This hands-off action (S4 — "delegating") would increase the probability that this behavior will either continue or become worse.

Situation Six

The parent has just returned from the hospital, where he or she has been recovering from an illness. During the parent's absence the family situation ran smoothly. The spouse at home was closely supervising the children during this time. The parent wants to maintain good behavior, but also wants to get the children involved in family decision making.

Diagnosis

The children have responded well over the last few months to the close supervision of the spouse. If the parent wants to maintain good behavior while increasing support and involving the children in family decision making, the best step is to maintain some direction and supervision, but give the kids opportunities for increased decision-making responsibility. If this responsibility is well handled, the children's behavior should be reinforced by increases in supportive behavior. This process should continue until the children are assuming significant responsibility for directing their own behavior.

Alternative Actions

The parent would:

D. Begin to let the children have some role in family decision making, but be careful that decisions made are carried out.

Rationale: (+2) This action (S2 — "selling") is the best approach to increasing the children's involvement in family decision making. Although some direction from the parent is maintained, support and responsibility are gradually increased by letting the kids participate more in decision making. If the children handle this involvement well, further increases in supportive behavior should follow.

B. Continue with close supervision and guidance.

Rationale: (+1) Although this style (S1 — "telling") would not involve the children in family decision making, it would tend to be a more appropriate initial action than decreasing direction and supervision too rapidly.

A. Do what can be done to make the children feel important and involved.

Rationale: (−1) Although the parent wants to begin to support and involve the children, this much supportive behavior might be too much too soon. As the children begin to demonstrate some ability to take responsibility, this action (S3 — "participating") would be more appropriate.

C. Let the children direct their own behavior.

Rationale: (−2) This hands-off action (S4 — "delegating") is too drastic a change from the close control the kids have become accustomed to and probably would be perceived as permissiveness. This action is only appropriate for very mature, responsible children who have demonstrated an ability to direct their own activities and provide their own support.

Situation Seven

Due to this parent's new job, work around the house needs to be shared in a different way. The children understand the problem and have made suggestions on how they could help. They have usually done their chores in the past.

Diagnosis

The children seem to be moderate to high in maturity, as demonstrated by their understanding, suggestions, and past behavior. Since a major change in how work is shared around the house is necessary and the children recognize this and are willing to pitch in, the parent's best action is to keep the channels of communication open and involve the children directly in any new work plans that have to be developed.

Alternative Actions

The parent would:

B. Participate with the family in deciding new ways to share the expanding responsibilities and support their cooperative efforts.

Rationale: (+2) This action (S3 — "participating") involves the children in developing the change and recognizes their maturity.

D. Just let the assuming of new responsibilities emerge; take no definite action.

Rationale: (+1) Once the strategy for the change has been developed and implemented with the involvement of the children, this action (S4 — "delegating") would be appropriate on a day-to-day basis.

C. Be willing to make new work assignments as recommended by the children, but make sure that everyone is doing his or her share.

Rationale: (−1) This behavior (S2 — "selling") would not fully utilize the children's potential to be involved in family decision making.

A. Tell the children what their new jobs are and then closely supervise the completion of those jobs.

Rationale: (−2) This action (S1 — "telling") would be inappropriate with a mature group of children. The problem is one of implementing a major change, not one of directing and supervising their behavior.

Situation Eight

The children are behaving in responsible ways and get along well with each other and their parents. Yet the parent feels somewhat unsure about his or her lack of direction and supervision of their activities.

Diagnosis

The children are very mature, as can be seen by their responsible behavior and good interpersonal relations with family members. The parent is projecting onto the children his or her own insecurities about what a parent "ought" to do — i.e, its an internal rather than external problem. Therefore, the parent's best action is to continue to let the children provide much of their own direction and support.

Alternative Actions

The parent would:

A. Stop worrying about it and continue to leave them alone.

Rationale: (+2) This action (S4 — "delegating") allows the children to continue to provide their own direction and socioemotional support.

D. Discuss the situation with the children and reach agreement on an action.

Rationale: (+1) At the present time, the children are behaving in responsible ways and are getting along well with family members. Thus, there is no clear reason why the parent needs to provide supportive behavior or engage in any special discussion with them (S3 — "participating").

B. Decide what action to take and then discuss the decision with the children.

Rationale: (−1) At this point, there is no indication of a need for a more directive or supportive style (S2 — "selling") with the children. The problem is one of parent insecurity. No parent intervention is needed.

C. Take steps to direct and supervise their behavior.

Rationale: (−2) This action (S1 — "telling") is totally unnecessary, since the children have already demonstrated responsible behavior.

Situation Nine

The children are way behind in some fall cleanup that the parent asked them to do around the outside of the house. Often, they don't show up when they are supposed to work.

When they do appear, rather than working, they play and fool around.

Diagnosis

The children are behaving very immaturely, as seen by their fooling around and poor attitude toward getting the outside cleanup done. Since time is running out for finishing the job, the parent's best action in the short run is to direct and closely supervise the completion of the cleanup.

Alternative Actions

The parent would:

C. Direct and closely supervise the children until the job is done.

Rationale: (+2) This action (S1 — "telling") provides the directive leadership needed to get the children to complete the cleanup.

B. Ask the children why the job is not getting done and listen to any suggestions they have, but supervise the completion of the job.

Rationale: (+1) This action (S2 — "selling") is appropriate for children of average maturity, which these children obviously are not. Thus, given the need to get the job done before winter sets in, supportive behavior is not necessary and may even encourage more fooling around.

D. Discuss the situation with the children in a friendly, supportive manner.

Rationale: (−1) This action (S3 — "participating") would reinforce the children's present immature behavior.

A. Let the children continue to set their own work schedule. They know what has to be done and will eventually get around to it.

Rationale: (−2) This hands-off action (S4 — "delegating") can only increase the probability that the children's "goofing off" will continue and the completion of the cleanup will be delayed further.

Situation Ten

The son, usually able to take some responsibility for handling money, is not responding to a change in spending caused by the family's present financial situation.

Diagnosis

The son is becoming less mature in the area of financial responsibility. This may be partly because the parent has recently limited spending. The parent's best move now is to keep communication channels open and get the son involved in the problem, while closely supervising him to be sure that the spending limits are observed. Positively reinforcing the son's recent decrease in maturity is likely to increase the probability that this behavior will continue in the future.

Alternative Actions

The parent would:

D. Discuss the problem with the son and answer questions on the family's situation, but see that he follows the new plan.

Rationale: (+2) This action (S2 — "selling") is the best approach in dealing with slippage in a normally responsible child. While communication channels are kept open, direction and supervision are maintained by seeing that the new spending limits are followed.

A. Allow the child involvement in determining the necessary spending limits and be supportive of his suggestions.

Rationale: (+1) This action (S3 — "participating") may become more appropriate as the child resumes his previous responsibility.

C. Avoid confrontation by not saying anything about his spending; leave the situation alone and assume it will all work out.

Rationale: (−1) This hands-off action (S4 — "delegating") will only increase the probability that this behavior will continue in the future.

B. Restate the new limitations to the son and then closely supervise his spending.

Rationale: (−2) This action (S1 — "telling") would be inappropriate for the son's present maturity level. Although some supervision and direction must be initiated, a "telling" style is too drastic for a child usually able to take responsibility for spending.

Situation Eleven

The parent's teenage daughter has been conscientious about doing her homework and helping around the house without supervision. Now that she is beginning to date, she seems to be on the phone much of the time and her schoolwork and chores are suffering.

Diagnosis

The daughter has not needed supervision from her parent in the past in the areas of homework and helping around the house. But now, with dating coming into the picture, she seems to be falling down in these responsibilities. The parent's best move with this normally mature girl is to discuss the situation with her and let her participate actively in trying to find a solution. When a solution is reached that is acceptable to all, her parent can once again leave her alone in these areas. The key factor here is to initiate a Style 3 ("participating") when the problem first begins, not months later. If the parent waits too long, he or she is likely to respond in anger and frustration and therefore go directly to a punitive "telling" style. This abrupt shift from "delegating" to "telling" can create hatred and hostility in the child.

Alternative Actions

The parent would:

B. Discuss the new development with the daughter and give her an opportunity to participate in the solving of the problem.

   Rationale: (+2) This action (S3 — "participating") allows the girl to come up with her own solution to the problem, but does not turn this responsibility over to her completely. While communication channels are kept open, some supervision is provided by talking with her and focusing her attention on the problem.

D. Don't intervene now; see if she realizes the problem and does something to correct it.

   Rationale: (+1) This action (S4 — "delegating") may have been appropriate with this mature girl in the past, but not now while she seems to be regressing. If the telephone problem is solved, the parent can move quickly back to this normally effective style.

C. Discuss the situation with the daughter and get her suggestions; then develop a plan she will have to follow.

   Rationale: (−1) This action (S2 — "selling") might be appropriate if the telephone problem continues after an S3 "participating" intervention. At this point, it would be too drastic a move for this normally mature child.

A. Restrict her phone calls and supervise the completion of her homework and chores around the house.

   Rationale: (−2) This action (S1 — "telling") would be too abrupt with such a generally mature child. It is likely to create unnecessary resentment.

Situation Twelve

Recently, the children seem to be upset with each other. Over the last several years they have gotten along well together. During that period of time, all the children have done extremely well in school and have taken responsibility for their chores around the house. They have worked in harmony together on family projects and have been able to settle any difficulties on their own.

Diagnosis

These children are very mature, as seen by their responsible and productive behavior over the last few years. The parent's best bet in the short run is to let the children try to resolve this present difficulty on their own. However, if the difficulty continues or intensifies, alternative leadership styles, particularly a "participating" (S3) style could be considered.

Alternative Actions

The parent would:

B. Not interfere; wait to see if the children work it out themselves.

Rationale: (+2) This action (S4 — "delegating") allows the children to come up with their own solution to the problem and maintain independence.

D. Discuss the situation with the children and be supportive.

Rationale: (+1) An S3 ("participating") intervention now might cause the children to become dependent on the parent for resolving any interpersonal problems they may encounter. It would become an appropriate intervention if the problem persists or intensifies, since that would indicate that the children need help in settling their disputes.

A. Talk with the children about the situation and then decide alone what needs to be done to remedy it.

Rationale: (−1) This action (S2 — "selling") is not appropriate at this time, since the children have the maturity to solve the problem themselves.

C. Act quickly and firmly to correct and redirect.

Rationale: (−2) This action (S1 — "telling") is too abrupt with such a mature group of children. The problem is one of interpersonal relationships, not direction and supervision.

References

Chapter One

1. This concept of "successful" versus "effective" was first suggested by Bernard M. Bass in *Leadership, Psychology, and Organizational Behavior* (New York: Harper & Brothers, 1960).
2. Amitai Etzioni in his *Comparative Analysis of Complex Organizations* (New York: The Free Press, 1961) presents an extensive discussion of the difference between position power and personal power. See also John R. P. French and Bertram Raven, "The Bases of Social Power," in Dorwin Cartwright and Alvin F. Zander, eds., *Group Dynamics*, 2d ed. (Evanston, Ill.: Peterson, 1960), pp. 607-620. In terms of what kids (or people) are like, Douglas McGregor makes a clear distinction between positive (Theory Y) and negative (Theory X) assumptions about people in his classic book *The Human Side of Enterprise* (New York: McGraw-Hill, 1960).
3. A. S. Neill, *Summerhill* (New York: Hart, 1960).
4. Francis L. Ilg and Louise Bates Ames, *Child Behavior* (New York: Harper & Row, 1972).
5. Benjamin Spock, *Baby and Child Care* (New York: Pocket Books, (1976), pp. 10, 11.
6. The PARENT-Self has been developed and adapted from the Leader Effectiveness and Adaptability Description (LEAD) instrument developed by Paul Hersey and Kenneth H. Blanchard at the Center for Leadership Studies. Both instruments are based on the theoretical frameworks presented in Hersey and Blanchard, *Management of Organizational Behavior: Utilizing Human Resources*, 3d ed. (Englewood Cliffs, N.J.: Prentice-Hall, 1977).

Chapter Two

1. An early attempt to develop a two-dimensional model was done at the Bureau of Business Research at Ohio State University. The two

behavioral dimensions they identified were "Initiating Structure" and "Consideration." See Ralph M. Stogdill and Alvin E. Coons, eds., *Leader Behavior: Its Description and Measurement*, Research Monograph No. 88 (Columbus, Ohio: Bureau of Business Research, The Ohio State University, 1957). Our directive behavior and supportive behavior dimensions are an outgrowth of this earlier work.
2. Situational Leadership Theory was developed by Paul Hersey and Kenneth H. Blanchard at the Center for Leadership Studies, Ohio University, Athens, Ohio, and at the School of Education, University of Massachusetts, Amherst. The Center for Leadership Studies is now located at 230 West Third Avenue, Escondido, California 92025. The most extensive discussion of the theory can be found in Hersey and Blanchard, *Management of Organizational Behavior*, 3d ed. (Englewood Cliffs, N.J.: Prentice-Hall, 1977).
3. Kenneth Blanchard was a faculty resource with Reverend Jesse Jackson at the February 1977 YPO (Young Presidents' Organization) University in Honolulu, Hawaii. The discussions of what he said at a luncheon session are taken from Blanchard's notes and do not represent his exact words.

Chapter Three

1. This concept of learning "a little bit at a time" is basic to the field of behavior management, reinforcement theory, or operant conditioning. In preparing the behavioral management aspect of this chapter as well as the next chapter, the most helpful reference for us was Lawrence M. Miller's well-written and easy to understand program text *Behavior Management: New Skills for Business & Industry* (Atlanta, Georgia, Behavioral Systems, Inc., 1976) and discussions with friend and colleague Bob Lorber of Continuing Education Corp. (of PSI) in Tustin, California.
2. Lloyd Homme, *How to Use Contingency Contracting in the Classroom* (Champaign, Ill.: Research Press, 1970). In this book Homme develops a process that he calls "contingency contracting." Much of this section was adapted from his material on "contingency contracting" and then integrated into Situational Leadership.
3. This concept of "positive contracts or contingencies" is derived from research by David Premack. As an example, see David Premack, "Toward Empirical Behavioral Laws: 1. Positive Reinforcement," *Psychological Review* 66 (1959): 219-233.
4. This example was taken from an enjoyable popular article by Alice Lake, "How to Teach Your Child Good Habits," *Redbook Magazine*, June 1971, pp. 74, 186, 188, 190.

Chapter Four

1. This motivation model first appeared in Paul Hersey and Kenneth H. Blanchard, *Understanding and Motivating Employees* (Athens, Ohio: Management Education and Development, Inc., 1968). For the most extensive presentation of the model, see Hersey and Blanchard, *Management of Organizational Behavior*, 3d ed. (Englewood Cliffs, N.J.: Prentice-Hall, 1977), Chapter 2.
2. Abraham H. Maslow, *Motivation and Personality* (New York: Harper & Row, 1954).
3. Frederick Herzberg, Bernard Mausner, and Barbara Synderman, *The Motivation to Work* (New York: Wiley, 1959); and Herzberg, *Work and the Nature of Man* (New York: World Publishing Co., 1966).
4. Lawrence M. Miller, *Behavior Management: New Skills for Business & Industry* (Atlanta, Georgia: Behavioral Systems, Inc., 1976).
5. Maslow, *Motivation and Personality*.
6. David C. McClelland discusses the importance of setting moderately difficult but achievable goals in his classic studies in *The Achievement Motive* (New York: Appleton-Century-Crofts, 1953).
7. J. Sterling Livingston, "Pygmalion in Management," *Harvard Business Review*, July-August 1969, pp. 81-89.

Chapter Five

1. This concept of the "regressive cycle" was first introduced in Paul Hersey and Kenneth H. Blanchard, *Management of Organizational Behavior: Utilizing Human Resources*, 3d ed. (Englewood Cliffs, N.J.: Prentice-Hall, 1977).
2. These guidelines are expanded and adapted from some "rules of effective punishment" developed by Lawrence M. Miller, *Behavior Management: New Skills for Business and Industry* (Atlanta, Georgia: Behavioral Systems, Inc., 1976).

Chapter Six

1. Thomas Gordon, *Parent Effectiveness Training* (New York: Wyden, 1970).
2. See William Oncken, Jr. and Donald L. Wass, "Management Time: Who's Got the Monkey?" *Harvard Business Review*, November-December 1974, pp. 75-80.
3. Eric Berne, *Games People Play* (New York: Grove Press, 1964).

4. See Thomas Harris, *I'm OK — You're OK: A Practical Guide to Transactional Analysis* (New York: Harper & Row, 1969); and Muriel James and Dorothy Jongeward, *Born to Win* (Reading, Mass.: Addison-Wesley, 1971). Abe Wagner was a faculty resource with Ken Blanchard at the May 1977 YPO (Young Presidents' Organization) University at Vienna, Austria. Abe lectured and distributed some mimeographed material on his approach to Transactional Analysis. Blanchard attended Abe's sessions and talked informally with him and found him very helpful in making TA "come alive."
5. Sigmund Freud, *The Ego and the Id* (London: Hogarth Press, 1927).
6. Eric Berne, *Principles of Group Treatment* (New York: Oxford University Press, 1964), p. 281.
7. Harris, *I'm OK — You're OK*.
8. A hand-out entitled "Transactional Analysis for the Supervisor/Manager" that Abe Wagner distributed at the YPO University at Vienna, Austria, May 1977, was very useful in this section.
9. Stephen B. Karpman, "Fairy Tales and Script Drama Analysis," *Transactional Analysis Bulletin* VII, No. 26 (April 1968), pp. 39-43.
10. James and Jongeward, *Born to Win*, pp. 82-83.
11. See Oncken and Wass, "Management Time: Who's Got the Monkey?"
12. Ibid., p. 76.
13. Ibid., p. 80.

Chapter Seven

1. The development of the PARENT instruments is based on Situational Leadership. This instrument was adapted from an earlier Hersey-Blanchard instrument, the LEAD (Leader Effectiveness and Adaptability Description). The first publication on LEAD appeared as Paul Hersey and Kenneth H. Blanchard, "So You Want to Know Your Leadership Style?" *Training and Development Journal*, February 1974.
2. The PARENT-Other is the same instrument as the PARENT-Self, but written so children, spouses, other parents, and so on can fill it out on a parent.

Chapter Eight

1. Joseph Luft and Harry Ingham, "The Johari Window, A Graphic Model of Interpersonal Awareness," *Proceedings of the Western Training Laboratory in Group Development* (Los Angeles: UCLA Extension Office, 1955). A more up-to-date version of the framework is presented in Joseph Luft, *Group Processes: An Introduction to Group Dynamics*, 2d ed. (Palo Alto, Calif.: National Press Book, 1970).

2. Sigmund Freud, *The Ego and the Id* (London: Hogarth Press, 1927).
3. Haim Ginott, *Between Parent and Child: New Solutions to Old Problems* (New York: Avon Books, 1965).
4. Kenneth Blanchard was a faculty resource with Alice Ginott at the February 1977 YPO (Young Presidents' Organization) University in Honolulu, Hawaii. The discussions of what she said at a session entitled "Between Parent and Child" are taken from Blanchard's notes and do not represent her exact words.
5. Wayne W. Dyer, *Your Erroneous Zones* (New York: Funk and Wagnal, 1976).
6. Wayne Dyer was also a faculty resource with Kenneth Blanchard at the February 1977 YPO University in Honolulu, Hawaii. Wayne told this story in one of his sessions there and it was taken from Blanchard's notes; it does not represent Wayne's exact words.
7. This sentence is adapted from a quotation by Dorothy Canfield Fisher that Wayne Dyer referred to in *Your Erroneous Zones*, p. 195.

Contributor Index

Ames, Louise Bates, 10
Bass, Bernard M., 4
Berne, Eric, 123
Blanchard, Kenneth H., 14, 24, 75, 76, 101, 147
Cartwright, Dorwin, 8
Coons, Alvin E., 21
Dyer, Wayne, 178-179
Etzioni, Amitai, 8
Fisher, Dorothy Canfield, 184
French, John R. P., 8
Freud, Sigmund, 122, 168
Ginott, Alice, 170-172
Ginott, Haim, 172
Gordon, Thomas, 117
Harris, Thomas, 122, 130
Hersey, Paul, 14, 24, 75, 76, 101, 147
Herzberg, Frederick, 81-85
Homme, Lloyd, 62
Ilg, Francis L., 10
Ingham, Harry, 168-173
Jackson, Rev. Jesse, 40-41
James, Muriel, 122, 141-42
Jongeward, Dorothy, 122, 141-42
Karpman, Stephen B., 139-41
Lake, Alice, 71
Livingston, J. Sterling, 95
Lorber, Robert L., 54
Luft, Joseph, 168-173
McClelland, David C., 95
McGregor, Douglas, 8
Maslow, Abraham H., 77-81
Mausner, Bernard, 81
Miller, Lawrence M., 54, 86-88, 110
Neill, A. S., 9
Oncken, Jr., William, 118, 143-44
Premack, David, 63
Raven, Bertram, 8
Spock, Benjamin, 10
Stogdill, Ralph M., 21
Synderman, Barbara, 81
Wagner, Abe, 122, 131-34
Wass, Donald L., 118, 143
Zander, Alvin F., 8